WORLD CUP 19[illegible]5

Edited by PETER BILLS

Editor of RUGBY WORLD magazine

HAMLYN

First published in Great Britain in 1995
by Hamlyn an imprint of Reed Consumer Books Limited
Michelin House, 81 Fulham Road, London SW3 6RB
and Auckland, Melbourne, Singapore and Toronto

ISBN 0 600 58585 9

A catalogue record for this book is available
from the British Library

Design Sue Michniewicz

Picture Research Jenny Faithfull

Production Juliette Butler

ACKNOWLEDGEMENTS

Rugby World would like to thank Bill Mitchell and Tony Pocock for their work on this project

PHOTOGRAPHIC ACKNOWLEDGMENTS

Front cover: Allsport main picture, top left, /Mike Hewitt top centre left, David Rogers bottom left, /Anton Want centre bottom left, **Back cover:** Allsport

Allsport 11 top, 12, 13, 18, 19 top, 19 bottom, 21, 27 top, 29 top, 30, 36 top, 36 bottom, 37 bottom, 39, 41 top, 47 bottom, 58, 67, 70 top, 71 top, 72, 73 bottom, 73 top, 74, 75 bottom, 75 top, 76, 77 bottom right, 77 top, /Agence Vandystadt/ Yann Guichaoua 25, /Agence Vandystadt/Richard Martin 20 bottom, /Agence Vandystadt/Eric Renard/Le Sport 20 top, /Shaun Botterill 22, /Simon Bruty 23 bottom, 26, /David Cannon 45 top, 45 bottom left, 50, 63, 69, /Chris Cole 64, /Mike Cooper 54, /Mike Hewitt 34, 53, /Ken Levine 31 bottom, /Clive Mason 38, 56, 57 top, 57 bottom, /David Rogers 1, 6, 24, 28, 29 bottom, 31 top, 32, 33 top, 33 bottom, 35, 37 top, 40, 41 bottom, 42, 43 top, 43 bottom, 44 top, 44 bottom, 45 bottom right, 46, 47 top, 48, 49 top, 49 bottom, 51, 52, 55 bottom, 55 top, 59, 60, 61 top, 61 bottom, 65 bottom, 65 top, 68, 70 bottom, 78, 79 bottom, 79 top, /Billy Stickland Inpho 10, 11 bottom, 14, 15 bottom, 15 top, 23 top, /Anton Want 27 bottom, 62, 66, 71 bottom, 77 bottom left.

Printed in Italy

Contents

Introduction

by Peter Bills
Editor, Rugby World Magazine

It has been a nerve-wracking business watching the alarming fluctuations that threatened preparations for the third rugby World Cup, scheduled to run from May 25 to June 24 throughout South Africa. They said it was premature to award the tournament to the country which, until comparatively recently, had been torn apart by warring political factions. At times, in the long build-up to kick-off day in Cape Town, such criticism seemed amply justified. And, even when Nelson Mandela strode nobly into power and South Africa turned its back at last on the evils of apartheid, other obstacles loomed in the path of the great rugby competition. Indeed, even quite recently, many wondered whether the infrastructure actually existed to host so huge an event in the new South Africa. Off-shore boats were planned to provide extra accommodation and the South African national airline ordered an extra fleet of aircraft to be hired to transport fans around the country.

But, for all that, the great event is now about to start. And there seems little doubt that the third World Cup will become far and away the most successful to date. The professional manner in which the tournament will be run may displease some, but it is manifestly clear that the sport world-wide badly needs substantial funds to boost its name and image. A lucrative, commercially supported World Cup can do so much to provide this facility. In this field, South Africa '95 will surely far outstrip any profits which might have been made from the first two World Cups.

There will be a feast of rugby, and conditions should be highly conducive to a fast, open, attacking game plan. Australia and the host nation, who kick-off the tournament, could conceivably meet again in the final. Many believe the ultimate winner will be one of them.

But, whatever the outcome and by whatever means, it is crystal clear that the game needs a tournament of riveting entertainment, a spectacle that will send a vibrant message around the world that Rugby Union, for all its painful deliberations over encroaching professionalism, is a sport of universal appeal and huge attraction.

THE QUALIFYING TOURNAMENTS

FOR THE 1995 WORLD CUP

The qualifying tournaments for the 1995 World Cup began in the autumn of 1992.

South Africa (the host nation) and the leading eight nations in the 1991 competition – Australia, England, New Zealand, Scotland, Ireland, France, Canada and Western Samoa – automatically qualified for the 1995 finals. The remaining seven places have been filled after a series of qualifying tournaments worldwide.

THE AFRICAN ZONE

NORTHERN TOURNAMENT

Date	Team	Score	Team	Score	Venue
26/10/93	**Tunisia**	**16**	**Ivory Coast**	**19**	(Tunis)
28/10/93	**Tunisia**	**5**	**Morocco**	**6**	(Tunis)
30/10/93	**Morocco**	**3**	**Ivory Coast**	**15**	(Tunis)

SOUTHERN TOURNAMENT

Date	Team	Score	Team	Score	Venue
3/ 7/93	**Kenya**	**7**	**Zimbabwe**	**42**	(Nairobi)
3/ 7/93	**Namibia**	**64**	**Gulf States**	**20**	(Nairobi)
7/ 7/93	**Kenya**	**9**	**Namibia**	**60**	(Nairobi)
7/ 7/93	**Zimbabwe**	**50**	**Gulf States**	**21**	(Nairobi)
10/ 7/93	**Kenya**	**24**	**Gulf States**	**23**	(Nairobi)
10/ 7/93	**Namibia**	**41**	**Zimbabwe**	**16**	(Nairobi)

PLAY-OFF TOURNAMENT

Date	Team	Score	Team	Score	Venue
14/6/94	**Morocco**	**17**	**Ivory Coast**	**9**	(Casablanca)
14/6/94	**Namibia**	**25**	**Zimbabwe**	**20**	(Casablanca)
16/6/93	**Morocco**	**9**	**Zimbabwe**	**21**	(Casablanca)
16/6/94	**Ivory Coast**	**13**	**Namibia**	**12**	(Casablanca)
18/6/94	**Morocco**	**16**	**Namibia**	**16**	(Casablanca)
18/6/94	**Ivory Coast**	**17**	**Zimbabwe**	**10**	(Casablanca)

Ivory Coast qualify

THE PACIFIC ZONE

Date	Team	Score	Team	Score	Venue
12/6/93	**Fiji**	**11**	**Tonga**	**24**	(Suva)
17/7/93	**Tonga**	**10**	**Fiji**	**15**	(Nukualofa)

Tonga qualify

THE AMERICAS ZONE

SOUTHERN TOURNAMENT

Date	Team	Score	Team	Score	Venue
26/ 9/93	**Chile**	**24**	**Paraguay**	**25**	(Santiago)
2/10/93	**Paraguay**	**3**	**Uruguay**	**67**	(Asuncion)
9/10/93	**Uruguay**	**14**	**Chile**	**6**	(Montevideo)
11/10/93	**Argentina**	**70**	**Chile**	**7**	(Buenos Aires)
16/10/93	**Argentina**	**51**	**Paraguay**	**3**	(Buenos Aires)
23/10/93	**Uruguay**	**10**	**Argentina**	**19**	(Montevideo)

NORTHERN TOURNAMENT AND PLAY-OFF

Date	Team	Score	Team	Score	Venue
12/3/94	**Bermuda**	**3**	**United States**	**60**	(Devonshire)
28/5/94	**United States**	**22**	**Argentina**	**28**	(Long Beach)
20/6/94	**Argentina**	**16**	**United States**	**11**	(Buenos Aires)

Argentina qualify

THE ASIAN ZONE

Date	Team	Score	Team	Score	Venue
22/10/94	**Malaysia**	**23**	**Sri Lanka**	**18**	(Kuala Lumpur)
22/10/94	**Japan**	**56**	**Taiwan**	**5**	(Kuala Lumpur)
23/10/94	**Singapore**	**5**	**Thailand**	**69**	(Kuala Lumpur)
23/10/94	**Hong Kong**	**17**	**South Korea**	**28**	(Kuala Lumpur)
24/10/94	**Sri Lanka**	**3**	**Japan**	**67**	(Kuala Lumpur)
24/10/94	**Taiwan**	**23**	**Malaysia**	**15**	(Kuala Lumpur)
25/10/94	**Thailand**	**0**	**Hong Kong**	**93**	(Kuala Lumpur)
25/10/94	**South Korea**	**90**	**Singapore**	**3**	(Kuala Lumpur)
26/10/94	**Malaysia**	**9**	**Japan**	**98**	(Kuala Lumpur)
26/10/94	**Taiwan**	**25**	**Sri Lanka**	**9**	(Kuala Lumpur)
27/10/94	**Singapore**	**13**	**Hong Kong**	**164**	(Kuala Lumpur)
27/10/94	**South Korea**	**65**	**Thailand**	**13**	(Kuala Lumpur)
29/10/94	**Hong Kong**	**80**	**Taiwan**	**26**	(Kuala Lumpur)
29/10/94	**Japan**	**26**	**South Korea**	**11**	(Kuala Lumpur)

Japan qualify

THE QUALIFYING TOURNAMENTS

THE EUROPEAN ZONE

EASTERN TOURNAMENT

1/5/93	**Germany**	**31**	**Lithuania**	**5**	(Berlin)
8/5/93	**Latvia**	**5**	**Germany**	**27**	(Riga)
24/5/93	**Russia**	**15**	**Georgia**	**9**	(Gdansk)
27/5/93	**Poland**	**23**	**Georgia**	**6**	(Gdansk)
29/5/93	**Lithuania**	**6**	**Latvia**	**7**	(Siauliai)
29/5/93	**Poland**	**5**	**Russia**	**41**	(Gdansk)
2/5/94	**Romania**	**60**	**Germany**	**6**	(Bucharest)
4/5/94	**Russia**	**69**	**Germany**	**5**	(Bucharest)
7/5/94	**Romania**	**30**	**Russia**	**0**	(Bucharest)

Romania qualify

CENTRAL TOURNAMENT

30/ 5/93	**Hungary**	**8**	**Israel**	**67**	(Budapest)
31/10/93	**Israel**	**10**	**Sweden**	**26**	(Den Haag)
31/10/93	**Holland**	**42**	**Czech Republic**	**6**	(Den Haag)
3/11/93	**Holland**	**56**	**Israel**	**0**	(Apeldoorn)
3/11/93	**Sweden**	**7**	**Czech Republic**	**34**	(Apeldoorn)
6/11/93	**Holland**	**31**	**Sweden**	**6**	(Amsterdam)
6/11/93	**Israel**	**0**	**Czech Republic**	**28**	(Amsterdam)
14/ 5/94	**Holland**	**33**	**Czech Republic**	**9**	(Brescia)
18/ 5/94	**Italy**	**104**	**Czech Republic**	**8**	(Viadana)
21/ 5/94	**Italy**	**63**	**Holland**	**9**	(Calvisano)

Italy qualify

WESTERN TOURNAMENT

10/10/92	**Andorra**	**3**	**Denmark**	**0**	(Andorra)
10/10/92	**Denmark**	**8**	**Switzerland**	**3**	(Andorra)
10/10/92	**Andorra**	**0**	**Switzerland**	**14**	(Andorra)
11/ 5/93	**Spain**	**40**	**Switzerland**	**0**	(Lisbon)
11/ 5/93	**Portugal**	**8**	**Belgium**	**3**	(Lisbon)
13/ 5/93	**Belgium**	**3**	**Spain**	**67**	(Lisbon)
13/ 5/93	**Portugal**	**32**	**Switzerland**	**0**	(Lisbon)
16/ 5/93	**Portugal**	**15**	**Spain**	**37**	(Lisbon)
16/ 5/94	**Belgium**	**42**	**Switzerland**	**3**	(Lisbon)
17/ 5/94	**Portugal**	**11**	**Wales**	**102**	(Lisbon)
21/ 5/94	**Spain**	**0**	**Wales**	**54**	(Madrid)
29/ 5/94	**Spain**	**35**	**Portugal**	**19**	(Madrid)

Wales qualify

EUROPEAN SEEDING TOURNAMENT

17/ 9/94	**Romania**	**9**	**Wales**	**16**	(Bucharest)
1/10/94	**Italy**	**24**	**Romania**	**6**	(Catania)
12/10/94	**Wales**	**29**	**Italy**	**19**	(Cardiff)

WALES join Group C with New Zealand, Ireland and Japan at the finals.

ITALY join Group B with England, Western Samoa and Argentina.

ROMANIA go to Group A alongside Australia, Canada and South Africa.

Wales's flanker, Hemi Taylor, tackles Romania's Traian Oroian in a European zone seeding match, won by Wales 16-9 in Bucharest

THE DRAW FOR THE 1995 FINALS

Thursday May 25	**Group A:**	**Australia v South Africa**	(Cape Town, 14.30)
Friday May 26	**Group A:**	**Canada v Romania**	(Port Elizabeth, 20.00)
	Group D:	**Scotland v Ivory Coast**	(Rustenburg, 16.00)
	Group D:	**France v Tonga**	(Pretoria, 18.00)
Saturday May 27	**Group B:**	**Western Samoa v Italy**	(East London, 13.00)
	Group B:	**England v Argentina**	(Durban, 17.00)
	Group C:	**Wales v Japan**	(Bloemfontein, 15.00)
	Group C:	**New Zealand v Ireland**	(Johannesburg, 20.00)
Tuesday May 30	**Group A:**	**South Africa v Romania**	(Cape Town, 14.30)
	Group B:	**Western Samoa v Argentina**	(East London, 12.30)
	Group D:	**France v Ivory Coast**	(Rustenburg, 18.00)
	Group D:	**Scotland v Tonga**	(Pretoria, 20.00)
Wednesday May 31	**Group A:**	**Australia v Canada**	(Port Elizabeth, 13.00)
	Group B:	**England v Italy**	(Durban, 17.00)
	Group C:	**Ireland v Japan**	(Bloemfontein, 15.00)
	Group C:	**New Zealand v Wales**	(Johannesburg, 20.00)
Saturday June 3	**Group A:**	**Australia v Romania**	(Stellenbosch, 15.00)
	Group A:	**Canada v South Africa**	(Port Elizabeth, 20.00)
	Group D:	**Tonga v Ivory Coast**	(Rustenburg, 13.00)
	Group D:	**Scotland v France**	(Pretoria, 17.00)
Sunday June 4	**Group B:**	**Argentina v Italy**	(East London, 13.00)
	Group B:	**England v Western Samoa**	(Durban, 20.00)
	Group C:	**New Zealand v Japan**	(Bloemfontein, 15.00)
	Group C:	**Ireland v Wales**	(Johannesburg, 17.00)

THE QUARTER-FINALS

Saturday June 10	**(E)**	**Winner D v Runner-up C**	(Durban, 13.00)
	(F)	**Winner A v Runner-up B**	(Johannesburg, 15.00)
Sunday June 11	**(H)**	**Winner B v Runner-up A**	(Cape Town, 13.00)
	(G)	**Winner C v Runner-up D**	(Pretoria, 15.00)

THE SEMI-FINALS

Saturday June 17	**(I)**	**Winner E v Winner F**	(Durban, 14.30)
Sunday June 18	**(J)**	**Winner G v Winner H**	(Cape Town, 14.30)
Thursday June 22		**Third place play-off**	(Pretoria, 14.30)

THE FINAL

Saturday June 24		**Winner I v Winner J**	(Johannesburg, 14.30)

1987 WORLD CUP

22 MAY - 20 JUNE

THE STORY

FINAL	**New Zealand**	**29**	**France**	**9**	*(Auckland)*
THIRD PLACE PLAY-OFF	**Australia**	**21**	**Wales**	**22**	*(Rotorua)*
SEMI-FINALS	**Australia**	**24**	**France**	**30**	*(Sydney)*
	New Zealand	**49**	**Wales**	**6**	*(Brisbane)*
QUARTER-FINALS	**Wales**	**16**	**England**	**3**	*(Brisbane)*
	Australia	**33**	**Ireland**	**15**	*(Sydney)*
	France	**31**	**Fiji**	**16**	*(Auckland)*
	New Zealand	**30**	**Scotland**	**3**	*(Christchurch)*

Halfway through the final of the first Rugby Union tournament ever to be played in a World Cup format, a rainbow spread across the sky behind Auckland's Eden Park. If ever a new competition had instantly become a symbol for a crock of gold at the end of the rainbow, then this surely was it.

This was the tournament the world had argued over for so many years, southern hemisphere pleas being met by that classic northern hemisphere reserve and caution for which the north remains famous (or should it be notorious?). But at last, on May 22 1987, New Zealand, the joint host nation with Australia, met Italy in the first ever World Cup game. The imbalance between a traditional power and one from an emerging rugby nation was emphasised, pretty brutally, by the All Blacks' 70-6 (or twelve tries to nil) demolition of the outsiders. No matter, it was a start, for both New Zealand and Italy; and of the two there was little doubt that the arrival of a World Cup competition would offer the greater opportunity for advancement to a nation like Italy.

It was appropriate that the first World Cup should be staged in the southern hemisphere. The impetus for the event had come from down under; indeed, the notion of the traditional Home unions being dragged kicking and screaming to the party was far from being fanciful.

If New Zealand were to dominate the tournament, that did not detract from the sheer pleasure and pride which many nations derived simply from being there. Fiji and Tonga represented the Pacific Islands, Fiji squeezing into the quarter-finals from Pool 3 at the expense of Argentina whom they beat in Hamilton. Both nations perished to New Zealand, Fiji by a stunning 74-13 margin though the Argentines did rather better by keeping the rampant home nation down to a winning margin of 46-15.

Pool 1 brought together Australia and England in the first match, and the Wallabies, misfiring like a badly stuttering motor engine, needed a highly doubtful 'try' by David Campese to help them get home by 19-6 in Sydney. Japan and the USA were the cannon fodder in this group although the Japanese hardly looked like lambs to the slaughter in restricting Australia to a 42-23 win.

Tonga lost every match in Pool 2, and Canada's rugby sun had not yet begun to rise back in 1987. So the group was decided between Wales and Ireland, the Welsh winning a scrappy game in Wellington by 13-6, with only one try scored in the match, by the Welsh centre Mark Ring.

Pool 4 was rather more competitive. France and Scotland were the heavyweights, and they were accompanied by Zimbabwe and Romania. The first two pool matches could not have been closer, Romania beating Zimbabwe 21-20 in Auckland while, on the same day in Christchurch, France and Scotland fought out a 20-20 draw! That meant, inevitably, that the side with the most tries would win the group and it would be crucial, because the second placed side would be faced with an horrendous task against New Zealand in the quarter-final. France scored 55 against Romania, Scotland 55 too! Scotland rammed 60 points down Zimbabwe's throats but, crucially, some defensive errors by the Scots allowed the southern Africans to score 21 points. Worse still, Scotland allowed Romania to score 28 points against them in their 55-28 victory in the final series of matches in the pool.

France, therefore, had a clear advantage when they met Zimbabwe in Auckland, for they knew what they had to do. In the event, France thrashed them 70-12 with Didier Camberabero creating a new world scoring record with 30 points in an international. Ironically, just hours earlier in Dunedin, Scotland's Gavin Hastings had set a then new world record with 27 points. His piece of history was to last just a matter of hours.

France finished the group having scored more tries than Scotland, so the first quarter-final paired New Zealand with Scotland in Christchurch. The match fulfilled all the Scots' worst fears. Long since denied their hugely influential and talented fly-half, John Rutherford, whose World Cup had lasted less than one full match because of an earlier knee injury sustained in an invitation event in Bermuda, Scotland had no answer to the intimidating combination of powerful forward play and cohesion, at pace, between forwards and backs in the New Zealand side. So a one-sided contest finished at 30-3 to New Zealand, bringing a sad end to the long and distinguished career of Colin Deans, who promptly retired.

The following day, in Auckland and Sydney, two more quarter-finals were decided. Australia raced away to a match-winning 24-0 lead in the first half against Ireland and then defended their total for a 33-15 win. Meanwhile, in Auckland, France and Fiji were weaving some delightfully entertaining patterns of running in a match of six tries which France won, fairly comfortably, by 31-16.

That left just England and Wales to contest the last place in the semi-finals. Their meeting at Brisbane was to have enormous consequences for the future of the game in England. With the Welsh badly disrupted by injuries England were expected to win. In the event, Wales were allowed to cast aside their obvious early doubts and surprise their opponents. Then they broke away to score the tries that won the match. England, against a side they should have crushed, were an embarrassment. They could not cope with some wily play by the line-out expert Robert Norster and the scrum-half Robert Jones. It was perhaps the most abject England performance ever, and it led directly to the departure of their coach Martin Green. When manager Mike Weston also left, England appointed Geoff Cooke to take up the job and Cooke's role in the renaissance of England's rugby was to be outstanding.

The sequel was startling. Welsh international rugby collapsed; England's revived gloriously.

POOL 1

Australia	**19**	**England**	**6**	*(Sydney)*
Japan	**18**	**USA**	**21**	*(Brisbane)*
England	**60**	**Japan**	**7**	*(Sydney)*
Australia	**47**	**USA**	**12**	*(Brisbane)*
England	**34**	**USA**	**6**	*(Sydney)*
Australia	**42**	**Japan**	**23**	*(Sydney)*

	P	W	D	L	F	A	Pts
Australia	3	3	0	0	108	41	6
England	3	2	0	1	100	32	4
USA	3	1	0	2	39	99	2
Japan	3	0	0	3	48	123	0

POOL 2

Canada	**37**	**Tonga**	**4**	*(Napier)*
Ireland	**6**	**Wales**	**13**	*(Wellington)*
Wales	**29**	**Tonga**	**16**	*(Palmerston North)*
Ireland	**46**	**Canada**	**19**	*(Dunedin)*
Wales	**40**	**Canada**	**9**	*(Invercargill)*
Ireland	**32**	**Tonga**	**9**	*(Brisbane)*

	P	W	D	L	F	A	Pts
Wales	3	3	0	0	82	31	6
Ireland	3	2	0	1	84	41	4
Canada	3	1	0	2	65	90	2
Tonga	3	0	0	3	29	98	0

POOL 3

New Zealand	**70**	**Italy**	**6**	*(Auckland)*
Fiji	**28**	**Argentina**	**9**	*(Hamilton)*
New Zealand	**74**	**Fiji**	**13**	*(Christchurch)*
Argentina	**25**	**Italy**	**16**	*(Christchurch)*
Fiji	**15**	**Italy**	**18**	*(Dunedin)*
New Zealand	**46**	**Argentina**	**15**	*(Wellington)*

	P	W	D	L	F	A	Pts
New Zealand	3	3	0	0	190	34	6
Fiji	3	1	0	2	56	101	2
Argentina	3	1	0	2	49	90	2
Italy	3	1	0	2	40	110	2

POOL 4

Romania	**21**	**Zimbabwe**	**20**	*(Auckland)*
France	**20**	**Scotland**	**20**	*(Christchurch)*
France	**55**	**Romania**	**12**	*(Wellington)*
Scotland	**60**	**Zimbabwe**	**21**	*(Wellington)*
France	**70**	**Zimbabwe**	**12**	*(Auckland)*
Scotland	**55**	**Romania**	**28**	*(Dunedin)*

	P	W	D	L	F	A	Pts
France	3	2	1	0	145	44	5
Scotland	3	2	1	0	135	69	5
Romania	3	1	0	2	61	130	2
Zimbabwe	3	0	0	3	53	151	0

1987 Semi-Finals

JUNE 13, SYDNEY

Australia 24 France 30

The first semi-final of the 1987 World Cup, played out between Australia and France, was probably the greatest competitive match ever played in the long history of the game. Comparisons between this semi-final and the 1973 game between the Barbarians and New Zealand are absurd. Only one thing links the two contests: the levels of skill on display. Of the rest, there can be no comparison. To produce so magnificent a spectacle of open, attacking rugby amid the pressure-cooker atmosphere of a World Cup semi-final was an outstanding, probably a unique, achievement.

So, at the tiny Concord Oval on the western side of Sydney, Australia and France fought out a game which will be remembered forever by those lucky enough to have been there. Many leapt up as though shot at the final whistle, their bodies shaking with tension and emotion. Six tries were rattled off by two teams which threw everything they possessed at each other. It made for compelling viewing,

The most dramatic moment of the 1987 World Cup. French full-back Serge Blanco celebrates his match-winning try, moments before the end of a wonderful semi-final against Australia

the kind of match which you simply could not stop watching for a single second. Australia, with the colossal advantage of playing in Sydney, were clear favourites. But the French had a back line of speed and magical creativity and intended to use it, at whatever cost. It was a high risk policy but one which was to succeed handsomely after a thousand frights and near misses.

With the match teetering at 21-21 deep in the second half, the French full-back Serge Blanco made the error which seemed as though it would cost his team the match. Caught up in the emotion of the play, Blanco ran out of defence and tried to beat one man too many. He was caught dangerously near his own line, attempted a hopeless pass to a colleague, and to prevent the try France infringed. Michael Lynagh landed the simple penalty-goal for a 24-21 lead to Australia which seemed to have settled, finally, the great game. But then, in the spirit of what had gone before, Didier Camberabero landed a difficult penalty-goal to level the scores once more at 24-all. The earlier scores, tries for Australia by David Campese and David Codey, both converted by Michael Lynagh, who also added three penalty-goals and a drop-goal, against tries for France by Lorieux, Sella and Lagisquet, which were all converted by Camberabero, who also added two penalties, seemed already an immense achievement. Yet we knew when Camberabero's second penalty flew high between the posts that none of those scores, splendid as they had been, would be enough to win the semi-final. More there had to be and more there was.

One of Australia's easier matches on the way to the semi-final was against USA whom they beat by 47-12 in Brisbane. Here the great David Campese has the beating of Gary Hein, the US wing, in a race for the ball

France had reached the final by heading their pool and then beating Fiji in the quarter-finals. In a France v Scotland pool game, John Jeffrey (left) grabs the ball for Scotland as France's hooker, Daniel Dubroca, is left powerless. France drew the game 20-20

The decisive moment came deep into injury time. Australia received possession and seemed capable of striking a serious blow even from way out. But Lynagh lost possession and Lagisquet hoofed the ball on. Lorieux reached the loose ball first and found support from the talented Charvet. Charvet was caught and the angle of the attack was again switched, its momentum maintained by bewildering handling under the fiercest pressure. Lagisquet and Rodriguez took it on amid the congested regions of a desperate Australian defence, before France's full-back was given the ball in a position some twenty-five metres from Australia's line. Blanco was by now physically exhausted and mentally shattered but he raised his body for one last grand effort. Not at his fastest as he headed for the corner, he moved agonisingly towards immortality as the

Australian cover, principally in the shape of hooker Tommy Lawton, dashed desperately across to try to reach him and save the score. In one dramatic moment, it seemed as though the whole sporting world had stopped for these two protagonists in their race for the corner flag. Inching his way ever closer, Blanco launched a despairing dive into the corner as Lawton dived too . . . a fraction too late. Blanco had scored, Camberabero swung over a magnificent conversion and France had won 30-24.

AUSTRALIA
Campese; Grigg, Slack *(capt)*, Papworth *(rep: Herbert)*, Burke; Lynagh, Farr-Jones; Lillicrap, Lawton, McIntyre, Cutler, Campbell *(rep: Codey)*, Poidevin, Miller, Coker

FRANCE
Blanco; Camberabero, Sella, Charvet, Lagisquet; Mesnel, Berbizier; Ondarts, Dubroca *(capt)*, Garuet, Lorieux, Condom, Champ, Erbani, Rodriguez

Referee: JB Anderson *(Scotland)*

JUNE 14, BRISBANE

New Zealand 49 Wales 6

The storm which Wales ran into on a balmy Sunday afternoon in June 1987 was to prove so powerful that it undermined the reputation of the national team for the next five years. Few of those who went to Queensland's famous headquarters, Ballymore, that day to see

After their heavy defeat by New Zealand in the semi-final, Wales came back strongly to beat Australia 22-21 in the third place play-off match in Rotorua. Here Richard Moriarty, the Wales captain, rules the line-out in that match

Paul Moriarty, the Wales flanker, breaks through the New Zealand defence in the semi-final. New Zealand won by 49-6

that World Cup semi-final, were expecting a public execution. Granted, Wales themselves were perhaps a bit surprised to be there, England having been favourites to reach the last four. But having disposed of their oldest and greatest enemy, Wales lined up against the New Zealanders in good heart, if not exactly peak condition.

But the events of the following eighty minutes were to prove shattering for Wales. The overwhelming defeat, by seven goals, a penalty-goal and a try to a solitary goal, added up to Wales's biggest ever defeat at that time. Their pack, weakened by injuries and the loss of vital players, was crushed in a contest which rapidly seemed like men against boys. New Zealand's quickest forward, Michael Jones, did not play because the match was on a Sunday and his religion frowned upon sport on the Sabbath. No matter, Robin Brooke-Cowden, Jones's temporary replacement, got virtually a free ride at open side as Wales were squashed into tiny morsels by the power of the All Blacks' pack.

The manner of their defeat was so humiliating that all Wales went into mourning. Within the next few years, key players who had endured that game – Jonathan Davies, John Devereux, Adrian Hadley, Richard Webster, David Young and Paul Moriarty – had all deserted Rugby Union for Rugby League. And, with others also signing professional forms, the heart was ripped out of Welsh international rugby. The effects of this disturbing trend were to be seen on Wales's tour of New Zealand the following year. Two Test matches were played and both resulted in hidings by 3-52 and 9-54. When the All Blacks visited Wales twelve months later, they won 34-9 but the climax of this disastrous run was in Australia, in 1991, when the Wallabies thrashed Wales 63-6 and New South Wales reached 70 points against them. All these stunning reverses could be traced back directly to the shattering World Cup semi-final defeat by the All Blacks in Brisbane.

Even the mercurial skills of Jonathan Davies were blunted in that 1987 semi-final match. It began as a slaughter and continued in the same pitiless manner. Devereux's try for Wales, converted by Paul Thorburn, made not a jot of difference in breaking the New Zealanders' remarkable flow. To round off a grim day, the Welsh lock Huw Richards was sent off.

NEW ZEALAND

Gallagher; Kirwan, Stanley *(rep: McCahill)*, Taylor, Green; Fox, Kirk *(capt)*; McDowell, Fitzpatrick, Drake, Pierce, G Whetton, A Whetton, Brooke-Cowden, Shelford

WALES

Thorburn; Evans, Devereux, Bowen, Hadley; J Davies, Jones; Buchanan, Phillips, Young, R Moriarty *(capt)*, Richards, P Moriarty, Collins *(rep: Sutton)*, P Davies

Referee: KV Fitzgerald *(Australia)*

1987 The Final

JUNE 20, AUCKLAND

New Zealand 29 France 9

The benefit of hindsight, that quality which turns fools into men of wisdom, suggests that the New Zealand side which won the 1987 World Cup was perhaps the finest that proud rugby nation has ever produced. Certainly there was an overall mastery about the '87 vintage, not only in the final against France but in earlier matches too, which lends credibility to the claim – despite the high excellence that has always marked New Zealand's rugby down the years.

The teams came to the match in very different frames of mind. For France even their own players were later to admit: 'Our final was against Australia.' They were in poor shape mentally for a final against New Zealand, seven days after their wondrous performance against Australia.

By contrast, all New Zealand sought only one thing – the glittering prize of the gold cup. It mattered not how they secured it, just whether it finished in All Black hands. The precision with which David Kirk and his team set about achieving that win was calm, confident and business-like. New Zealand possessed great power up front in players such as Shelford, the Whetton brothers and the front-row men Fitzpatrick and McDowell. At half-back, to channel operations, they had Kirk's wisdom and intelligence allied to Fox's playmaking skills, based on kicking.

The All Blacks could spread their game, too, through Gallagher, Kirwan, Stanley and Taylor. They chose not to do so in the final, to any serious extent, because the pressure of the occasion stifled much of their attacking skills. But Fox out-manoeuvred France with his tactical kicking. It pinned the French into their own territory for long spells and the awesome strength of the All Black forwards ensured an endless supply of possession for the New Zealand No. 10. Fox's goal-kicking gradually turned the screw on the Frenchmen, and the All Blacks' power in the loose was phenomenal.

The French, facing the wind in the first half, limited New Zealand's lead to 9-0 at half-time. Fox dropped a goal and then, in attempting another, saw the ball miscue miles wide. But a wicked bounce fooled the defence and set up a try for breakaway Michael Jones, the fastest open-side flanker the game had seen for years. Others followed, from Kirk who scored from close range after supporting a burst by Jones and from Kirwan, a powerful runner who finished off a sixty-yard

John Kirwan scores for the All Blacks against France in the 1987 final

David Kirk scores and the World Cup is within touching distance for the All Blacks

break by Kirk which Shelford had supported, before putting the wing over for his sixth try of the tournament. Fox was not at his imperial best in place-kicking terms for he could convert only one of the tries. But crucially he punished the mistakes France increasingly made as the pressure was first maintained and then mounted, to land four penalty-goals. Those kicks tore the heart out of the French.

France's back-line was a flying machine, from Lagisquet on the wing to Sella and Charvet at centre and Blanco at full-back, and the open attacking game which they had wanted to play proved impossible in the face of the All Blacks' defensive disciplines. The Australian referee, Kerry Fitzgerald, by no means saw all their misdemeanours but the trend of the match condemned France to increasing frustration. The scrum-half, Pierre Berbizier, scored their only try late in the game but by then it was apparent that they would lose. Camberabero converted Berbizier's try and added a penalty-goal but the image was of New Zealand drawing away to an inevitable win with the brave but tired French unable to change the nature and result of the final.

At the end, the New Zealand captain, David Kirk, received the trophy to the delight (and relief) of an entire nation. It had simply meant so much to the All Blacks and the whole of New Zealand that no other outcome could be contemplated. Their coach, Brian Lochore, had withstood the intimidating pressure and had quietly moulded together a pack of forwards which was without peer, not only in this World Cup but anywhere in the world at that time. It was not always going to be so easy and straightforward for the New Zealanders, as they were to discover four years later. Perhaps that is why it was only later, after Lochore had long since gone, that the real worth of his 1987 winners really came to be understood. They were a magnificent side of many talents, professionally prepared and well coached. They were the first to grasp the value of the new World Cup.

NEW ZEALAND
Gallagher; Kirwan, Stanley, Taylor, Green; Fox, Kirk *(capt)*; McDowell, Fitzpatrick, Drake, Pierce, G Whetton, A Whetton, Jones, Shelford

FRANCE
Blanco; Camberabero, Sella, Charvet, Lagisquet; Mesnel, Berbizier; Ondarts, Dubroca *(capt)*, Garuet, Lorieux, Condom, Champ, Erbani, Rodriguez

Referee: KV Fitzgerald *(Australia)*

The French flanker, Eric Champ, bursts upfield in the final against New Zealand, won easily by the All Blacks 29-9 in Auckland

1991 WORLD CUP

OCTOBER 3 - NOVEMBER 2

THE STORY

FINAL	**Australia**	**12**	**England**	**6**	*(Twickenham)*
THIRD PLACE PLAY-OFF	**New Zealand**	**13**	**Scotland**	**6**	*(Cardiff)*
SEMI-FINALS	**Scotland**	**6**	**England**	**9**	*(Murrayfield)*
	Australia	**16**	**New Zealand**	**6**	*(Dublin)*
QUARTER-FINALS	**New Zealand**	**24**	**Canada**	**13**	*(Lille)*
	France	**10**	**England**	**19**	*(Paris)*
	Scotland	**28**	**Western Samoa**	**6**	*(Murrayfield)*
	Ireland	**18**	**Australia**	**19**	*(Dublin)*

Throughout the rugby grounds of Britain, across the Irish Sea to Dublin and the English Channel to France the action blurred into a month-long fiesta. The watching world was gripped by the occasion, and the staging of the second World Cup, played for the first time in the northern hemisphere, was a supreme success. It took rugby forward miles from the first event staged in Australia and New Zealand four years earlier.

There was drama, consequence and vivid action from first to last. Argentina's meeting with Australia, before the packed, nostalgic stands of Stradey Park, Llanelli, produced a little gem of a game in crisp autumn sunshine. It was the occasion that made it; knowledgeable rugby folk turned out in their thousands to enjoy good rugby by some of the world's greatest stars. And that trend was to be continued for most of the four weeks of the competition.

Defeat by the All Blacks in the first match of the tournament meant that England were condemned to a long, tortuous path if they wished to reach the final. If, as anticipated, things turned out according to the form book, then the second-placed side in Pool 1 would almost certainly have to take on France in Paris. Serge Blanco, great elder statesman of French rugby, had doused that potential fire with petrol months earlier after the England-France Five Nations game at Twickenham, won 19-15 by England. 'I feel sorry for England if they do not beat New Zealand in the World Cup's first game', Blanco had intoned. 'For they will have to come to Paris in the quarter-final and that will end their interest in the event.' Or words to that effect . . .

Neither Italy nor USA could prevent the inevitable occuring in Pool 1 and it was the same story in Pool 2, where Scotland and Ireland dominated Japan and Zimbabwe. So the meeting of the Scots and Irish in Edinburgh decided the group. Ireland seemed on course for an upset until their full-back, Jim Staples, was savagely hit by the Scottish breakaway Finlay Calder when attempting to take a high kick. It changed the course of the match for when the groggy Staples spilled another kick Scotland poured through to score. The match had been turned on its head and the Scots went on to seize a 24-15 victory, giving them a home quarter-final against Western Samoa while Ireland went back to Dublin to prepare for the Australians.

The Aussies had won Pool 3, but only after a hard-fought 9-3 win over the surprise side, Western Samoa, conquerors of Wales. Argentina, fancied by many, finished with three straight defeats. The decisive moment in this pool came thirty-five seconds after half-time in the Wales-Western Samoa match. With the score still at 3-3, despite the physical battering the Welsh had taken, their scrum-half Robert Jones raced back to touch down a kick by a Samoan player over Wales's line. Jones dived for the ball together with Vaega, the Samoan wing, and, though subsequent TV replays of the incident showed that it was the Welshman who reached the ball first, the French referee, Patrick Robin, some thirty yards away, awarded a try. The buoyant Samoans went on to take a shock 16-13 win and help put out the Welsh.

In Pool 4, no one could halt France's inexorable progress towards a home quarter-final in Paris but it was Canada, against all expectations, who accompanied them into the last eight after spirited victories over Fiji and Romania. They pushed France close, too, losing by only 13-19 in Agen. The Canadians could go no further, although in their quarter-final New Zealand had to work hard to repel another bold Canadian challenge in the lashing rain at Lille, by 29 points to 13. It had been a great tournament for the unfancied Canadians.

Meanwhile, twenty-four hours earlier, there had been a game of seismic proportions in Paris. England won it, just, and only very late on after French discipline had cracked as spectacularly as an orange bursting under intense pressure. There was never much between the sides but in the bull-ring atmosphere of the Parc des Princes England's forwards were magnificent. Skinner's tackle which drove back the big French No. 8 Cécillon will be remembered for years.

In the end, England won because they maintained their iron discipline to the end, allowing Carling to score a crucial try and Webb to land a vital last-minute penalty. Nine points in the last five minutes by England snatched the game away from the broken-hearted French. The New Zealand referee, David Bishop, afterwards caught the full ire of the French coach, Daniel Dubroca, in an incident which led, some time later, to Dubroca's resignation.

Scotland, meanwhile, were ending the Western Samoan fairy story 28-6 at Murrayfield, the big tackles of the islanders insufficient to upset a determined Scotland side in front of its own fans. And so to Dublin where the last quarter-final was the best, indeed perhaps the most dramatic match of the whole month-lông tournament.

Australia led, early on, and seemed in control through Campese's two super tries and Lynagh's goal-kicking. But suddenly, after they had seemed only just able to hang on to the game, Ireland snatched a dramatic try out of nothing. An Australian movement broke up in midfield and the Irish flanker, Gordon Hamilton, seized the ball and set off for Australia's line. In a flash, the inspiration of the Irish caught fire. To a man, Lansdowne Road rose to roar Hamilton home, and the try, well converted, gave Ireland an 18-15 lead. The upset of the entire World Cup was just three minutes away.

But it was in those few remaining minutes that Australia's pedigree shone through. Ireland made the mistake of not hoofing the ball out of play to waste precious seconds and when the Wallabies did win the ball, they needed only one attempt to strike the killer blow. Lynagh spun the ball down the back line and then popped up himself out on the wing to dive into the corner for the winning score. Australia had snatched a dramatic 19-18 win in the final seconds, and the World Cup had a match to remember forever.

POOL 1

England	**12**	**New Zealand**	**18**	*(Twickenham)*
Italy	**30**	**USA**	**9**	*(Otley)*
New Zealand	**46**	**USA**	**6**	*(Gloucester)*
England	**36**	**Italy**	**6**	*(Twickenham)*
England	**37**	**USA**	**9**	*(Twickenham)*
New Zealand	**31**	**Italy**	**21**	*(Leicester)*

	P	W	D	L	F	A	Pts
New Zealand	3	3	0	0	95	39	9
England	3	2	0	1	85	33	7
Italy	3	1	0	2	57	76	5
USA	3	0	0	3	24	113	3

POOL 2

Scotland	**47**	**Japan**	**9**	*(Murrayfield)*
Ireland	**55**	**Zimbabwe**	**11**	*(Dublin)*
Ireland	**32**	**Japan**	**16**	*(Dublin)*
Scotland	**51**	**Zimbabwe**	**12**	*(Murrayfield)*
Scotland	**24**	**Ireland**	**15**	*(Murrayfield)*
Japan	**52**	**Zimbabwe**	**8**	*(Belfast)*

	P	W	D	L	F	A	Pts
Scotland	3	3	0	0	122	36	9
Ireland	3	2	0	1	102	51	7
Japan	3	1	0	2	77	87	5
Zimbabwe	3	0	0	3	31	158	3

POOL 3

Australia	**32**	**Argentina**	**19**	*(Llanelli)*
Wales	**13**	**Western Samoa**	**16**	*(Cardiff)*
Australia	**9**	**Western Samoa**	**3**	*(Pontypool)*
Wales	**16**	**Argentina**	**7**	*(Cardiff)*
Wales	**3**	**Australia**	**38**	*(Cardiff)*
Argentina	**12**	**Western Samoa**	**35**	*(Pontypridd)*

	P	W	D	L	F	A	Pts
Australia	3	3	0	0	79	25	9
Western Samoa	3	2	0	1	54	34	7
Wales	3	1	0	2	32	61	5
Argentina	3	0	0	3	38	83	3

POOL 4

France	**30**	**Romania**	**3**	*(Beziers)*
Fiji	**3**	**Canada**	**13**	*(Bayonne)*
France	**33**	**Fiji**	**9**	*(Grenoble)*
Canada	**19**	**Romania**	**11**	*(Toulouse)*
Fiji	**15**	**Romania**	**17**	*(Brive)*
France	**19**	**Canada**	**13**	*(Agen)*

	P	W	D	L	F	A	Pts
France	3	3	0	0	82	25	9
Canada	3	2	0	1	45	33	7
Romania	3	1	0	2	31	64	5
Fiji	3	0	0	3	27	63	3

1991 Semi-Finals

OCTOBER 26, MURRAYFIELD

Scotland 6 England 9

Glittering it most certainly was not, glorious manifestly it was. No rugby match consisting of four penalty-goals and a drop-goal could really be termed a classic. And yet this World Cup semi-final, which drew together the game's oldest enemies for a place in the final, was a gem. It was a match played before 60,000 fervent supporters, the great majority of them Scots. And for England to have survived another journey into the cauldron, after their quarter-final victory over France in Paris only seven days earlier, was a phenomenal achievement.

Scotland had a side to make difficult the lives of any opponents. Their great threat was around the fringes of the scrum where Jeffrey, Calder and White in the back row formed an outstanding partnership with the tough, nuggety Gary Armstrong at scrum-half. With back-row men like that and the whole Scottish side fired with pride, England knew they faced another harrowing examination.

The winning kick. The England fly-half, Rob Andrew, drops the goal that won the World Cup semi-final by 9-6 against Scotland in Edinburgh

They were not surprised at what ensued. From scrum to line-out, in loose play and down the backline, the snarling Scots did their best to mount an impenetrable barrier to England's aspirations. England, fielding a huge and powerful pack, gleaned the better quality possession but fly-half Andrew inevitably kicked most of it, either to touch or to put up the high bomb to test the Scots' defence. However, England's back-row defence was of such a high order, their tackling so consistently excellent, that the Scots were frustrated. Given this factor and the line-out superiority of Ackford and Dooley, England gained a slight but discernible advantage.

Yet the commitment was of such intensity that neither side could break through for what one imagined would have been the decisive try. And so it came down to goal-kicking. Scotland led 6-0 early on through two Gavin Hastings penalty-goals before Webb replied with penalties of his own, after thirty-four and fifty-seven minutes. Then came the story of the match – the tale of the two kicks. The first, with the scores tied at 6-6, came when England infringed no more than twenty yards from their line with only eighteen minutes of the match remaining. If Hastings could kick it, Scotland would take a psychologically crucial 9-6 lead with time fast running out. A place in the World Cup final would beckon.

And yet somehow, inexplicably, Hastings missed it. His rhythm appeared the same as before, his preparation identical. He looked calm and unflustered, casual even – perhaps too casual. Somehow, agonisingly for Scotland, the ball was fired wide of an upright and England escaped . . . to

Gavin Hastings lines up the comparatively easy and crucial penalty in the semi-final against England. Inexplicably, Hastings shot wide

work their way down to the other end of the field, and for Andrew to drop a snap goal to snatch the lead for England with just seven minutes left. It was Andrew's fifteenth drop-goal for England which equalled the world record. As time began to run out, Andrew knew his kick had won the semi-final for England.

In those two acts, the semi-final was probably decided. Yet England might have made more of their forward supremacy, especially in the set scrums. They could have moved the ball further out to danger men such as Guscott and Rory Underwood. Instead, they opted for safety and a place in the final. It was understandable, given the fear that one dropped pass in the back line would have offered a voracious Scottish back row the scraps on which to create a try.

England had reached the semi-final after a bitter struggle against France in Paris in the quarter-final. Here the New Zealand referee David Bishop lays down the law to captains Will Carling and Serge Blanco as the match boils over

It was a tight, tense semi-final, the quintessential 'winner takes all' contest. To have come through two such severe tests as those mounted by France and Scotland in their own backyards, brought great credit to the England side.

SCOTLAND
G Hastings; Stanger, S Hastings, Lineen, Tukalo; Chalmers, Armstrong; Sole *(capt)*, Allan, Burnell, Gray, Weir, Jeffrey, Calder, White

ENGLAND
Webb; Halliday, Carling *(capt)*, Guscott, Underwood; Andrew, Hill; Leonard, Moore, Probyn, Ackford, Dooley, Skinner, Winterbottom, Teague

Referee: KV Fitzgerald *(Australia)*

Grant Fox lines up another penalty for the All Blacks in their semi-final against Australia. Australia won 16-6

OCTOBER 27, DUBLIN

Australia 16 New Zealand 6

Australia, searching for revenge for their failure at the 1987 World Cup, relieved the All Blacks of their world crown with a brilliant and compelling exhibition of attacking rugby in a marvellous match in the Irish capital. Leading the way for the Wallabies was the mercurial David Campese. No more than six minutes of the semi-final had gone when Australia won fast, second-phase ball in a dangerous position around the New Zealand 22. But instead of fly-half Lynagh taking the scrum service, Campese appeared from nowhere to catch the pass and slice in a curving arc across and then through the All Blacks' cover for a dramatic try in the corner.

Six minutes later, Lynagh added a penalty-goal, followed in twenty minutes by another piece of Campese magic. The Wallaby wing shot away down the right and when his path to the line was blocked, he threw an instinctive pass inside him. The Australian centre Horan had supported Campese's run and now held the high pass at lightning speed to cross for a brilliant try. Lynagh converted but missed three other chances of penalty-goals which could have put Australia 20 points clear at the interval. Instead, in the final moments of the half, Fox landed a penalty for the hitherto outplayed All Blacks to make it 13-3 at half-time.

Once into the second half, it was Australia's turn to feel the pressure as New Zealand raised their game in a desperate attempt to retain the coveted cup. They began to secure copious amounts of quality possession, forcing the Australians onto deep defence. In midfield, none did better to repel constant raids than the Wallaby centres, Horan and Little.

Lynagh gave the tired and battered Australians some breathing space with a sixty-first-minute penalty-goal to make the score 16-3, and in truth that was crucial. Although Fox then kicked his

The quarter-finals had seen what was perhaps the most exciting match of the whole tournament, Ireland v Australia in Dublin. It was Michael Lynagh's crucial try in the corner that robbed Ireland of a famous win

The 1991 World Cup had begun with a match between the holders, New Zealand, and the host country, England, at Twickenham, the All Blacks emerging victorious by 18-12. Ian Jones, the New Zealand No. 4, leaps high as the line-out goes the All Blacks' way

second penalty of the match, New Zealand were too far behind to close the deficit. Australia, sensing a place in the final was now in their grasp, made no mistakes in the final quarter. And they richly deserved their win. They had played with passion, intensity and high skill which had delighted the Dublin crowd of almost 55,000. The Wallabies had proved that it was possible to be attack-minded in a semi-final and emerge victorious just as they had done, so memorably, in the semi-final four years earlier. Campese, as so often, had lit the touch paper but others, including every forward, had played a handsome role. So Australia were through to a final against England at Twickenham, perhaps the outcome that the majority of fans had hoped for.

AUSTRALIA
Roebuck; Campese, Little, Horan, Egerton; Lynagh, Farr-Jones *(capt)*; Daly, Kearns, McKenzie, McCall, Eales, Poidevin, Ofahengaue, Coker

NEW ZEALAND
Crowley; Kirwan, Innes, McCahill, Timu; Fox, Bachop; McDowell, Fitzpatrick, Loe, I Jones, G Whetton *(capt)*, A Whetton, Carter, Brooke

Referee: JM Fleming *(Scotland)*

1991 The Final

NOVEMBER 2, TWICKENHAM

England 6 Australia 12

England, having moved heaven and earth to get past the redoubtable French in Paris and the wily Scots in Edinburgh by playing a tight, highly disciplined game, based almost entirely on the power of their huge pack, suddenly tore up the script for the final. Astonishing as it may seem, England decided that they could not take those tactics into the final before the biggest watching world audience ever known to the game. And so they adopted a game plan which involved spreading the ball down the back line at almost every opportunity. Such tactics played into the hands of the grateful Australians.

Will Carling grabs Australia's Marty Roebuck but not before he gets his kick away in the final

Before the game, the Wallabies had labelled England's play boring and declared that they had not played rugby of the same class as themselves. This was undoubtedly true, in the sense that the Aussies had produced free flowing rugby high in entertainment. But people tend to remember only winners in cup finals. They have little recollection of losers who have played bravely and thrillingly, yet ultimately lost the cup. And that was to be England's fate at Twickenham on that dramatic November day.

England dominated the Wallabies up front and monopolised possession. But when they sent the ball down the back line nothing happened. England had built their success of previous years on their giant pack. While it would be wrong to say that their backs had become superfluous, they had certainly been under used. And threequarters not accustomed to handling the ball are rarely very effective when they are given it. As David Kirk said later: 'Although they did run the ball around effectively, the last pass went to ground; the positioning wasn't quite right. A few mistakes here and there, a missed pass, a dropped pass, a wrong option wins and loses finals. Australia played the way they played throughout the tournament. England played a new style and it is difficult to be precise with a new style on the big occasion.'

Defeat must have broken the hearts of a magnificent pack. Ackford and Dooley were superb in the line-outs, the back row of Skinner, Winterbottom and Teague was in roaring form and the front row never buckled, hooker Moore even finding time to make a considerable contribution in the loose. With that base, England ought to have won. But their backs ran prettily yet totally ineffectively because they ran across the field. The Australian drift defence simply moved sideways to bar their way.

Skipper Will Carling had to accept much of the blame. Given the failure of the England backs to break through in the first half with so much ball, Carling ought to have changed tactics and played to the pack after half-time. Their power could have won it. But Carling, never a great tactician, changed nothing and England continued to batter at the green and gold jerseys, to no effect. Wallabies such as Horan, Little and the back-row men were giants in defence. Their captain, Nick Farr-Jones, said: 'England are not quite as good when the ball does get wide because they are not sure what to do in those situations.' That said it all.

Australia were unlucky not to take the lead in the twenty-fourth minute when only a cruel bounce of the ball denied Campese a try from a kick ahead. But Lynagh quickly landed a penalty for a 3-0 lead before the Wallabies scored the only try of the final. It began for them in deep defence with England pressing. The centre, Tim Horan, was first to a loose ball but, instead of hacking it into touch, saw the opportunity and sprinted away up the touchline. He kicked only when the cover threatened to close him down and found touch just a few yards from the England line. Too late, England recognised the danger. Ofahengaue won the line-out, the Aussies drove off the back and Daly was driven over the line, with his fellow prop

Tony Daly, the Australian prop, is driven over the England line shortly before half-time for the only try of the final

McKenzie, for the vital try. Lynagh converted for a 9-0 half-time lead.

England lost another chance of points when Andrew missed a drop but Webb, having missed two first-half penalties, finally landed a goal with twenty minutes left. Alas for England, Lynagh soon replied in kind to stretch the lead to 12-3 and, although Webb landed another goal, England's predictable play behind the scrum was insufficient to breach Australia's defence.

The contest was full of drama right to the final whistle, with England only needing one converted try to send the game into extra time. But that score never materialised and the Australians lifted the glittering trophy, merit indeed for their entertaining attacking play which they had sustained right through the tournament. The Wallabies, a fine side and excellent ambassadors for the game, ran out worthy winners. The tragedy for England was that by dint of their magnificent forwards they could and should have won the cup. Living with that knowledge will, forever more, be desperately difficult for the Englishmen.

The Wallaby captain, Nick Farr-Jones, lifts the World Cup in triumph

ENGLAND
Webb; Halliday, Carling *(capt)*, Guscott, Underwood; Andrew, Hill; Leonard, Moore, Probyn, Ackford, Dooley, Skinner, Winterbottom, Teague

AUSTRALIA
Roebuck; Campese, Little, Horan, Egerton; Lynagh, Farr-Jones *(capt)*; Daly, Kearns, McKenzie, McCall, Eales, Poidevin, Ofahengaue, Coker

Referee: WD Bevan *(Wales)*

LION

Pool A

AUSTRALIA	**The current holders ended 1994 in good form and many critics back them to retain the Cup**
CANADA	**If they get the basics right and play to their considerable potential, Canada could do well**
ROMANIA	**Drawn in the so-called group of death, they are the rank outsiders**
SOUTH AFRICA	**They have enormous talent and will prove hard to beat in their own land**

Australia start as firm favourites to win this pool. With the retirement of Nick Farr-Jones, their captain in 1991, and handicapped by a string of injuries which have taken out such key players as Lynagh, Eales, Ofahengaue and Horan at one time or another during the build-up to 1995, Australia have seized the opportunity to introduce no fewer than twenty-one new caps, a number of them young players of high quality, such as George Gregan, Ilie Tabua and David Wilson. Now the Wallabies look as strong as ever.

South Africa, in contrast, who open the tournament against them in Cape Town on May 25, look unsettled. They have used three coaches since 1992 and have experimented with no fewer than sixty-one players in various key positions. They can play thrilling rugby but their frenetic activity since their re-admission to international competition has not been put to profitable use. Even halfway through their 1994 tour of Wales, Scotland and Ireland there was no clear indication of the players likely to make up their World Cup squad.

Canada beat Romania 19-11 in 1991 in their pool match. It began their run of success which took them to the quarter-finals and earned them the respect of the whole rugby world

(opposite) **South Africa's outstanding lock, Mark Andrews, holds on to the ball in their 1994 Test against Argentina**

Canada, the third side in Pool A, are emerging fast as a committed rugby nation but may not be strong enough to repeat their triumphs of 1991. However, they are likely to use some promising youngsters such as Mike James, John Hutchinson, the powerful wing David Lougheed and the No. 8 Colin McKenzie. Canada have never met Australia in international competition and they will not be intimidated by them in any way.

On the face of it, few would give the fourth team in the pool, Romania, much hope of winning any of their three pool matches. But they are a big, physical side and if they could start believing in themselves a bit and begin attacking with the ball in hand, employing their quick wingers, they just might cause an upset.

Australia

Greg Campbell

FIXTURES

V	**SOUTH AFRICA** May 25, Cape Town 14.30
V	**CANADA** May 31, Port Elizabeth 13.00
V	**ROMANIA** June 3, Stellenbosch 13.00

The day after the Wallabies' epic 1991 World Cup final win over England at Twickenham, the Australian players sauntered onto the team bus, heading for Gatwick and the long flight home to Sydney. Their reserve centre Anthony Herbert was carrying the case containing the Webb Ellis Cup. As a hotel guest walked by, Herbert asked him: 'Have you met "Bill"?' After carefully taking the gold trophy from the case, Herbert said proudly: 'We're taking "Bill" home.'

For just over two years, "Bill" travelled the length and breadth of Australia. The cup was won by Australians for Australians and it was only right that the whole country should have the opportunity to see at first hand the prize that twenty-six rugby players had devoted years of their lives to winning. "Bill" is rugby's Holy Grail.

The Webb Ellis Cup will now be on offer again in South Africa and, as defending champions, the Wallabies seem certain to be installed as favourites. Given their eighteen victories from twenty-two Tests since the 1991 World Cup, that is not an unfamiliar situation for the Australian team. But now it is "Bill" who is up for grabs.

As defending champions, the Wallabies automatically qualified for the tournament but that is where the easy road ended. None of the visiting fifteen countries would have wanted a first-up encounter against the host team, – the Springboks. But somehow the Wallabies drew the short straw and the 1995 World Cup will kick-off in Cape Town with the Wallabies lining up against the Boks at Newlands Stadium. Clearly it is a match which will shape the Wallabies' World Cup destiny.

Of the 1991 World Cup XV, full-back Marty Roebuck, winger Rob Egerton, No. 8 Troy Coker, flanker Simon Poidevin and the captain, Nick Farr-Jones, have all retired leaving notable holes in the champion team. In addition, serious injuries have sidelined

John Eales, the Wallabies' powerful young lock, rises above the line-out in the South Africa v Australia Test in Cape Town in 1992

Tim Horan bursts past four South Africans in the Australia v South Africa Test in Sydney in 1993

lock John Eales, fly-half Michael Lynagh, centre Tim Horan and flanker Willie Ofahengaue for months at a time.

In previous years, it has been the lure of Rugby League contracts which has stripped the Wallaby team of its stars but now it has been misfortune. The Australians have been forced once again to dig deep down for new resources, and they have unearthed some gems in Ilie Tabua, George Gregan and David Wilson among the startlingly high number of twenty-one new caps who have been introduced into the Wallaby team since the beginning of the 1992 season.

George Gregan, barely 5ft 6in and weighing only 10 ½ stone, had an astonishing game for Australia in the 1994 Bledisloe Cup in Sydney. He brought off a shuddering tackle on Jeff Wilson to prevent what would have been New Zealand's winning try four minutes from the end of the match and had already dumped the All Blacks' formidable prop, Richard Loe, and their lock, Mark Cooksley, with equally crushing tackles. On balance, coach Bob Dwyer is buoyed by his findings although the injury toll at the time was a severe frustration for it happened just as he was trying to mould his team under the new ruck and maul laws. Now Dwyer readily admits that the need to blood new talent was a blessing in disguise: 'These injuries have seen us (the selectors) give players the opportunity to play at Test level which they may not have received under normal circumstances. And it has been great to see players such as Tabua, Gregan, Howard and Bowen come through.'

Following back-to-back losses to the All Blacks and the loss to South Africa in the first Test in 1993, it was being asked whether sweeping changes were needed to the team in order

David Campese, Australia's hero in 1991, heads for the line

George Gregan, Australia's highly promising scrum-half, is one of the twenty-one discoveries who have made their debut since 1992

to defend successfully the next World Cup. The second Test against the Springboks at Ballymore became a watershed match and the Wallabies responded magnificently to the pressure and the challenge and scored a memorable 28-20 win. Dwyer made no secret of the fact that players' careers were on the line. 'It was a statement of fact. There was pressure on everyone including the coach. The third Test decider proved to be our best performance since the World Cup. Ian McIntosh, then the South African coach, said to me after the game, "You gave us a rugby lesson today".'

Dwyer nominates that performance, the second half against South Africa at Newlands in 1992, the second Test against France in 1993 and the record, blitzing win by 73-3 over Western Samoa in 1994 as the only times the Wallabies have managed to play near their best since 1991. He believes the chief reason for their disappointing play was their inability to arrange training-camps, especially in the off season. 'Unlike other countries we have been forced to rely on three-day assemblies before a Test. The camps are absolutely essential as they keep the team together and maintain a focus,' says Dwyer. In fact, the Australian RFU later accepted the importance of training-camps in their defence of the World Cup and made arrangements to hold four camps in successive months from November through to February this year. The plan was that these would be followed by two Tests against Argentina in early May 1995.

Dwyer nominates the busy domestic representative itinerary as a further problem. He says: 'It's been more of a physical than a mental strain because of the number of top-level games which are now played, such as the Super-10 tournament. There were some players who were dragging their bums around when we played Ireland and Italy and then were jumping out of their skins when we played Western Samoa. The 1992 season wasn't so bad because all the players were still hyped up after the World Cup. But, in saying that, I don't think we played tremendously well.'

Having drawn South Africa first-up in the Cup the Wallabies will be well prepared for what will be in store for them at Newlands on Thursday, May 25. Over the past three years, the Wallabies have played the Springboks four times for three victories, including a superb record-breaking 26-3 win at Newlands. 'But they will be a huge hurdle for us,' Dwyer has said, 'more than when New Zealand played England in the opening match in 1991, because the South Africans are more fanatical. It is a big benefit for us to have played them in 1992. We are now aware of some of the variables associated with a Test against the Springboks in Cape Town which can be a distraction.'

Canada looms as Australia's other main pool opponent and the Canucks are fast developing a high respect for themselves around the rugby world – particularly after qualifying for the 1991 quarter-finals and their victories over Wales and France in 1993 and 1994. When the Wallabies travelled to Canada on their way to France in late 1993 they scored a comfortable 43-16 win in Calgary. Leading up to the Cup, the Canadians embarked on an impressive preparation with away Tests arranged against France, England and Scotland followed by a short Test-match visit to New Zealand.

However, despite this build-up, Dwyer is not convinced that the Canadians will be able to repeat their excellent 1991 results: 'That year they had a very good team. I'm unsure whether they can assemble similar players next time around. They had a good forward pack that had mobility and toughness which was surprising for an emerging rugby nation.'

The Wallabies' third pool match will be against Romania, whom they have never played before. 'I watched them on video when they played France in 1993 and they appear to have a mobile pack with most of their forwards more or less the same size,' he recalls.

In 1991 the Wallabies' four key players were Eales, Lynagh, Horan and Campese, who was regarded as the star of the whole tournament. Indeed, so important was his contribution to the Wallabies' World Cup drive that Farr-Jones has often said that his team would not have won the Cup had Campese not been on hand. He will again figure prominently in 1995. His attacking vision remains sharp and imaginative while his daring inspiration has given team mates the courage to play with additional flair.

Lynagh played in only seven out of Australia's last sixteen Tests up to the end of 1994 but Dwyer remains con-

Willie Ofahengaue

On his day he is probably the most dynamic breakaway forward in world rugby. Born in Tonga, he went to Australia and his outstanding ability was recognised by Bob Dwyer, the Wallaby coach, who introduced him to international rugby in 1990 in the Test series against New Zealand. The strong impression he made in those matches established him as a fixture in the side and he was a member of Australia's World Cup winning team of 1991. Ofahengaue was troubled by injury during a lengthy period which stretched from 1993 into 1994 but will surely be a major contributor when the Wallabies begin their defense of the World Cup against South Africa in Cape Town at the end of May.

Michael Lynagh

has now passed a phenomenal 800 points in international rugby for Australia. He made his debut in their Grand Slam tour of the UK and Ireland in 1984, playing at centre with Mark Ella at fly-half. When Ella retired, Lynagh moved inside to fill the No. 10 shirt and has been there ever since. An outstanding goal-kicker, he has improved immeasurably as a reader of the game and took over from Nick Farr-Jones as Australia's captain in 1992. Injuries restricted his appearances in 1994 but he is expected to lead Australia again in the World Cup in South Africa.

vinced that his captain is still the best fly-half in the world. 'We need Michael to play like the player of 1991 and as he did on the French tour in 1993. He's been badly hit with injuries and illness but I have no doubt he is still the best in the world.'

Although he was only twenty-one in 1991, the impact and contribution Eales made to Australia's triumph was extraordinary. He was without peer in the line-out, he moved about the field like a panther and his tackling was decisive – just check with Rob Andrew. Dwyer believes Eales didn't produce his best form last year after missing the entire 1993 season because of a severe shoulder injury but still rates him one of the world's best players.

The blooding of twenty-one new caps plus the recovery from injury of players such as Lynagh, Ofahengaue, Eales and possibly Horan has vastly improved the Wallabies' overall depth. But as Dwyer comments: 'The key is also to keep improving at the top end as well.' He is delighted that the IRB decided to change again the experimental ruck and maul law after he was an outspoken critic of the original change in 1992. He says the new adjustment has re-emphasized the importance of the scrum and saved the prop from possible extinction. 'The art of scrummaging has been given due importance again and recognised as an essential part of the game of rugby, ' he says.

The Wallabies know the road to retaining the World Cup will be even harder than it was four years ago. The standard of competition throughout the world has risen since 1991, as they realised when struggling to beat Italy in Australia in a two-match Test series in 1994. Italian rugby especially has come on by leaps and bounds in recent years, no doubt helped by the outstanding Australian and New Zealand players who winter there. 'It will take a very high level of performance and a minimum of bad luck over the period of the Cup to win it,' says Dwyer cautiously.

And as for 'Bill', there are still a few regions of Australia which need to be covered and the Wallabies are keenly focused to make a series of appearances after June 24 for their much valued travelling companion.

Canada

Peter McMullan

The Canadian view of what lies ahead is typical of a nation where confidence is an accepted characteristic. The pool draw for the 1995 World Cup could scarcely be more demanding – Romania followed by the 1991 champions Australia and then the hosts South Africa – but they're still talking of a quarter-final place.

FIXTURES

V ROMANIA
May 26, Port Elizabeth 20.00

V AUSTRALIA
May 31, Port Elizabeth 13.00

V SOUTH AFRICA
June 3, Port Elizabeth 20.00

Norm Hadley, Canada's giant lock, now playing in England with Wasps, dominates the line-out against France in the 1991 World Cup

As one of the quarter-finalists from 1991, and thus an automatic inclusion in the 1995 draw, Canada will surely be viewed in a very different light from the squads that took the Maple Leaf to New Zealand and then to France. Unknowns at the inaugural event in 1987, the Canadians made real waves with an opening 37-4 rout of Tonga, in Napier, followed by spirited losses to Ireland and Wales.

Four years on it was a very different story. Victory over Fiji, by 13-3 at Bayonne, and Romania, by 19-11 in Toulouse, opened the door to the quarter-final. Then France won a contentious pool finale by 19-13, in Agen, before the holders New Zealand were more than relieved to come away from rain-lashed Lille with a 26-13 result. There the Canadians earned worldwide acclaim for a thunderous second-half effort rewarded by tries from scrum-half Chris Tynan and flanker Al Charron.

Both those players continue as high-profile members of the Canadian national team and, barring injury, are sure of squad places for May and June. Equally confident, too, should be seven other veterans of the Lille encounter – full-back Scott Stewart, a wing on that occasion, wing now centre Steve Gray, outside half Gareth Rees, who played centre in 1993, along with loose-head prop Eddie Evans, lock Norm Hadley, and Gord MacKinnon and Glenn Ennis, partners with Charron in a magnificent back row. Tight-head Dan Jackard missed the All Blacks through injury but was soon back and a first-choice selection.

Together they provide coach Ian Birtwell with an essential nucleus of experience. Birtwell, a fisheries biologist with the federal government, has been Canada's coach since late 1989. 'There is no question that, with suitable preparation and physical conditioning, Canada can compete with any nation. Nevertheless the task facing us in the World Cup is immense and we will have to be even fitter than we were in France in 1991. Obviously fitness is going to be a priority. We have lost some players since the last World Cup but we have gained in experience and have been able to introduce a number of younger players to the squad. If we get the basics right and play to our potential we will do very well,' he says.

Rees, second only to the full-back and 1991 captain Mark Wyatt as Canada's leading scorer, with 202 points to Wyatt's 263 from twenty-nine Tests, concurs with Birtwell's opinion:

Canada celebrate after Ian Stuart scores the first try against Wales at Cardiff in 1993

'I believe Canada can go even further than we did in 1991. We know we can beat the best in the world: we proved it by beating Wales and France in 1994. Australia will be difficult but South Africa have never played Canada and will not intimidate us in any way.' A prolific goal-kicker, Rees, like Ennis, has played in all seven of Canada's World Cup games to date. He says: 'If we do get through to the quarter-finals we will be on such a high that I would not bet against us on the day.'

As was to be expected, a number of promising newcomers have made their names since 1991. They include the young lock Mike James, who did so well in the 18-16 upset of France in June 1994, just before France won both Tests in New Zealand, and wings Winston Stanley, a new cap against the USA last year, and Ron Toews, first capped in the 26-24 victory over Wales in Cardiff in November 1993. Others to make a mark since 1991 include flanker John Hutchinson, who provided a superb effort in Cardiff, the powerful wing David Lougheed and the dynamic No. 8 Colin McKenzie.

David Speirs, the hooker at Lille, and lock John Robertsen retired after the 1991 tournament but returned to senior club rugby in September 1994 and could challenge for further caps. Both of Canada's 1987 World Cup hookers, Karl Svoboda and Mark Cardinal, are still very much in the picture. John Graf, who appeared at scrum-half against Romania in 1991, and has been capped also at outside half, centre and wing, is another name to remember, as is Ian Stuart, now playing strongly at inside centre, who was admired by all as Canada's robust first-choice scrum-half in 1987.

Since 1991 both Stuart and Svoboda have been winning Canadian captains, as was Hadley against the USA in 1992. He joined Wasps, of London, from Suntory, of Tokyo, at the start of 1993-94 but then suffered a severe leg fracture that sidelined him until the start of the 1994-95 season. His return to full fitness and mobility plus the excellent form he is showing for Wasps could go a long way to restoring the essential power and stability of the Canadian scrum, while enabling him to challenge his two successors for the captaincy in South Africa.

Gareth Rees, second only to the 1991 captain, Mark Wyatt, as Canada's leading scorer with 202 points to Wyatt's 263, has played in all seven of Canada's World Cup games to date

Romania

FIXTURES

V	**CANADA** May 26, Port Elizabeth 20.00
V	**SOUTH AFRICA** May 30, Cape Town 14.30
V	**AUSTRALIA** June 3, Stellenbosch 13.00

Romania picked up the World Cup draw card that no one wanted. To be paired in a group with the holders Australia, host nation South Africa and the wily Canadians would be no one's idea of fun. Losing the European play-off zone matches against Wales and Italy condemned Romania to make up the numbers in the desperately difficult Pool A, playing in Cape Town, Port Elizabeth and Stellenbosch.

On the face of it, few would give the Romanians much hope of winning any of their three pool games. They start by meeting Canada, then play South Africa and finish by taking on the champions, Australia, in Stellenbosch on June 3. But not all Romania's recent opponents believe the form book will necessarily prove an accurate indicator of what they will achieve in South Africa in May and June 1995.

Daniel Neaga, Romania's scrum-half, passes out in Romania's seeding match against Italy, won by Italy 24-6 in Catania

The Welsh lock forward, Phil Davies, says: 'The Romanians are no mugs. They could push Canada close when they meet. As it will be the first match the two sides play in the World Cup, a lot could depend upon preparation and who gets that right. I certainly wouldn't write off the Romanians' chances of pulling off an upset in that one. But it's pretty unlikely they could hold up Australia or South Africa so it's hard to see them reaching the quarter-finals. They are in a tough group but could go close against Canada.'

Davies says the Romanians must try to expand their game plan before they start their World Cup campaign. When they met Wales in the heat of Bucharest for the important qualifying match, the home side gave the Welsh plenty to think about in terms of securing the ball. But when it came to using it Romania's hopes started to decline.

The outside half Nichitean kicked too much, and not with enough accuracy to unravel a workmanlike Welsh

Romania's Nicolae Fulina races towards the line in their seeding match against Italy in Catania

defence. He looks a tidy and competent player though he doesn't send the ball such long distances as Ignat, the former Romanian outside half, used to do. And although there was some obvious pace on both the Romanian wings, in Colceriu and Solomie, they did not receive anything like enough chances to really test the Welsh. As Georges Coste, the coach of Italy, observed: 'If Romania had had a cool head to work out what to do with the ball they won, Wales would have been blown away. The Romanian pack will pose problems to a number of sides.'

Phil Davies agrees, saying: 'The Romanians have big forwards who can win good ball. At the moment, Canada would appear to have a little more flair outside the scrum but, should the Romanians try to attack more with the ball in their hands, they could test Canada. The Canadians lost to us in the summer, and if Romania improve the Canadians could have a job holding them. Romania are a big, physical side. They have tall lads in the back five of their pack and that gives them obvious advantages and plenty of options in the line-out. But given the size of them, I was a bit disappointed with their scrummage. It was too loose. I thought it would be much more of a test for us.

They would also be a more effective side if they spread the ball wide from time to time. They appear to have threequarters who are capable of direct running and must learn to use them in the World Cup.

'At the moment, they are too predictable. But their pack has real possibilities. The forwards picked up and drove well against us and we had to put in a lot of tackles. One other thing they need is more self-belief. The Canadians won't lack that so the Romanians must improve in that respect. But overall they will be an awkward proposition for any team they meet because they have the size and capacity to win some ball. Any side that does that will have a chance. Romania just need to work on developing their game.'

After the 6-24 defeat by Italy in their second qualifying match, the Romanian coach, Mircea Paraschiv, will surely understand that they must use the ball constructively. With strong forwards like Leonte, Cojocariu and Ciorescue, all three of whom have been battle-hardened in French senior club rugby, he has men who should be able to examine even the most redoubtable of opponents. But even their efforts will count for nothing if the side is not using its head and not using the ball. Against England, in a damp and chilly Twickenham, where they lost by 3-54 last November, their backs were largely ignored and their pack outplayed.

Mike Hall, the Cardiff centre, breaks through the Romanian defence, in the Wales v Romania European seeding match, won by Wales 16-9 in Bucharest

South Africa

Dan Retief

FIXTURES

V	**AUSTRALIA** May 25, Cape Town 14.30
V	**ROMANIA** May 30, Cape Town 14.30
V	**CANADA** June 3, Port Elizabeth 20.00

If strength in depth were the only yardstick the Springboks would be odds on to win the World Cup. More to the point, they now appear to have a much more settled squad and will certainly play with absolute commitment.

Their record in the thirty months since the new era of Springbok rugby started with a Test against the All Blacks at Ellis Park in August 1992 suggests that South Africa possesses playing resources as rich as the gold seams which underpin the country's economy. During that time their profligate selectors have awarded Springbok colours to no fewer than seventy-seven players, with fifty-six of them gaining full Test caps. Few countries have the capacity to select what amounts to virtually four different Test teams in such a short space of time. But all the numbers game indicates is simply that South Africa has a large number of quality players and that their passion for rugby is undiminished.

South Africa's frenzied activity since their re-admission to international rugby has not been put to profitable use. Though the basis of a good side emerged from their tour of Wales and Scotland in 1994 there is still no clear indication of how the bulk of their World Cup squad will be made up. Whereas most observers can name the majority of the twenty-six players whom Australia, New Zealand, France and England will take to the World Cup there are very few Springboks who can expect, with absolute certainty, to make the team.

South Africa has employed three coaches – John Williams, Ian McIntosh and Kitch Christie – since 1992 and such has been the pressure on the men in charge to produce victories that very little in the way of specific planning and

Andre Joubert, South Africa's outstanding full-back, races away to score in their 1993 Test against Australia in Sydney

preparation for the World Cup has taken place. With each defeat has come greater panic – in spite of the fact that South Africa chose to play the top nations in their quest to regain former glories – with the players simply straws to be clutched at in the hope of some improvement. Thus South Africa in eighteen Tests leading up to the tour to Wales, Scotland and Ireland capped twelve props, eleven locks, eleven flankers, six hookers, six scrum-halves, ten centres and five full-backs in the hope that another man might do better than the last instead of allowing a player to grow into the role. South Africa's intense programme also led to many players suffering serious injuries, thus contributing to the lack of continuity.

That autumn tour of 1994 under Kitch Christie, a man known for his painstaking planning, became a last-ditch effort to establish a settled squad of players for the World Cup. Christie and Francois Pienaar, the current captain, have a relationship which started in rugby and has extended into a business partnership. The coach would be aware that the captain believes the biggest problem for his team has been haphazard selection. 'It is very difficult to build confidence and reliability when every game is like a trial,' said Pienaar. 'I am convinced that the fear of being dropped has contributed a great deal to our inability to play as a team.'

Pienaar is the one man who can expect to be in Cape Town when the Springboks assemble for their opening match against Australia at Newlands on May 25. Although he has had to endure much criticism, Pienaar's assured and mature handling of his team on overseas tours has eventually won him the respect he deserves. At the same time his stature as a player and leader has grown immeasurably, to the extent that he is now seen as vital to South Africa's hopes of success.

Well aware that the biggest problem for South Africa in the Tests played during the last two and a half years has been the inability of the forwards to seize dynamic control, Christie has been

Helpful hands appear to be lifting the Springboks' lock, Mark Andrews, in the line-out in South Africa's Test against Argentina, 1994

Jacques Olivier, one of South Africa's several fast and aggressive wingers, had an excellent game in the 1992 Test against England at Twickenham

forced to take some extraordinary steps, such as plucking the tight-head prop Tommie Laubscher from his farm at the age of thirty-one to make his Test debut. The lock Drikus Hattingh also benefitted from the quest for tight forward solidity, while the swing through the British Isles was used to find the best combination of South Africa's many outstanding loose forwards – with Pienaar given a bigger role in the line-out. The realisation that most leading international sides play conservative, territorial rugby dictated by a kicking fly-half also brought re-instatement for Joel Stransky instead of the exciting runner Hennie Le Roux though in the

South Africa's lock, Drikus Hattingh, wins the ball in a line-out against England at Twickenham in 1992

event Le Roux regained favour and played instead of Stransky in both Tests.

South Africa possesses an abundance of big, strong and fast backs such as Pieter Muller, Japie Mulder, Brendan Venter, Thinus Linee and Christian Scholtz, speedy and creative wings in Chester Williams, Chris Badenhorst, Jacques Olivier and Pieter Hendriks (hopefully James Small as well) and a distinguished pair of full-backs in Andre Joubert and Gavin Johnson.

The challenge will be to find a pack with the strength and size to provide consistent primary possession and the fitness to play at the required tempo. Other players, such as the big lock Mark Andrews, the injured Hannes Strydom and the promising young props Ollie Le Roux and Marius Hurter from Northern Transvaal, may also come into the reckoning.

Although South Africa's three leading provinces – Transvaal, Orange Free State and Western Province – will be involved in the Super-10 tournament ahead of the World Cup, Christie is hopeful that the World Cup squad will be given some respite from the rigours of this competition. He would like his squad to gather for regular training before taking on Western Samoa in two warm-up internationals late in April. South Africans are hoping that Christie will by then have come up with the best fifteen of the many who could wear the green-and-gold.

In the pool matches, Romania should give South Africa no trouble and, with home advantage, it would be surprising if the Springboks failed to beat Canada. Australia is their main obstacle obviously, and if they lose that game, things may start to become a little difficult for them. They would almost certainly have to meet England in the quarter-finals and if England can adopt a successful running game they may well have the better of South Africa. Only if the Springboks win the pool competition will they face comparatively easy opposition in Italy or Argentina in the quarter-finals.

Francois Pienaar

has proved himself a strong, inspirational captain of the South African side. He survived the desperately disappointing tour of New Zealand in which the Test series was lost 2-0 to bring the Springboks to Wales and Scotland. His storming displays on that tour enhanced his reputation as a powerful, driving loose forward on the blind side. The Transvaal player made his international debut in the 1993 Test series against France.

Hennie Le Roux

is an unorthodox stand-off for arguably his least successful attribute is his kicking. Another player from the Transvaal side to graduate to international rugby, he made his Test debut in the same match as Pienaar, against the 1993 French side. He has fought hard for the Test No. 10 shirt against the likes of Joel Stransky and Natal's Henry Honiball. He is a tremendous running, attacking stand-off able to break the gain line and also launch his line speedily and effectively. Though Stransky was included in the Springboks' squad for the 1994 tour of Wales and Scotland as the first-choice fly-half, because it was thought that a kicker rather than a runner was needed, Le Roux regained favour, displaced Stransky and played storming games in both Tests.

Pool B

ARGENTINA	**Left behind a little by other emerging nations, they seem unlikely to reach the quarter-finals**
ENGLAND	**The pool matches are no problem, but later on Australia, New Zealand and South Africa may halt them**
ITALY	**They played brilliantly against Australia in 1994 and may cause an upset in South Africa**
WESTERN SAMOA	**Thrashed by Australia in 1994, a quarter-final place may be beyond them**

England should have no problem in heading Pool B. Western Samoa, Argentina and Italy do not look nearly good enough to threaten a major upset against the 1991 finalists. But the winner of Pool B will have to meet the runner-up in Pool A in the quarter-finals, who will be either South Africa or Australia. At that point things start to look difficult for England.

The main problem facing Jack Rowell, the England coach, is that he probably took over from Geoff Cooke twelve months, or even two years, too late in the context of winning the 1995 World Cup. England have started to show that they recognise a need for change but the process cannot be achieved overnight and Rowell is left with difficult decisions to make about the make-up of the front row, the back row, about the outside half and probably about the full-back too.

Rafael Bullrich of Argentina passes out of the scrum during the South Africa v Argentina Test, September 1994

(opposite) **Wayne Proctor, the Wales winger, leaps above Italy's Arancio in the last of the European seeding matches, won by Wales 29-19 in Cardiff**

Argentina had a difficult 1994 tour of South Africa, losing both Tests. They won the South American championships, not althogether convincingly from Uruguay, but have an unsettled squad. If they reach the quarter-finals, they will probably look back on 1995 as the year of a successful World Cup for them.

Italy are not complete outsiders in Pool B because they have made remarkable progress as an emerging rugby nation. Their performance against Wales at Cardiff in the European seeding competition was disappointing but when at their best, as against Australia on tour in 1994, they can play brilliant rugby.

It seems unlikely that Western Samoa can equal their great triumph of 1991. Though they beat Wales during the latter's South Seas tour in 1994, their heavy defeat against Australia in the same year must have badly shaken their confidence.

Argentina

Eric Weil

Argentina know they must replace their conservative, forward-orientated game with more imaginative and attacking rugby if they are to reach the quarter-finals and make a real impression on the World Cup.

FIXTURES

V	**ENGLAND** May 27, Durban 1700
V	**WESTERN SAMOA** May 30, East London 1230
V	**ITALY** June 4, East London 1300

Although the Argentine Pumas won four internationals within a month in mid-1994, nobody was really satisfied, although all these matches had been hard fought and close. The two narrow Test wins (by 16-15 and 19-17) in Buenos Aires came against what was virtually Scotland's A team, and the two Tests against the United States (won by 28-22 away and 16-11 at home) were expected to be a lot easier. The Pumas have not quite woken up to the fact that during the last decade other 'secondary' rugby-playing countries have narrowed the gap with the top-level nations faster than Argentina has done.

Earlier qualifying games, during the South American Championship in 1993, were won easily enough against Paraguay (51-3) and Chile (70-7), but then Argentina got a shock against surging Uruguay – a decisive game for the title and this a qualifying place for the World Cup. Uruguay led them 10-9 when a number of incidents almost stopped the game. Had that happened and had the precedent of earlier decisions been followed, the game would have gone to Uruguay. But play continued and the Pumas eventually won by the reasonable margin of 19-10.

The Argentine RU president, Lino Pérez, says: 'The best Argentine team I have seen was that of 1985-86. Since then we have not progressed technically and have been left behind both in international matches and club rugby. We play an old-fashioned game and must try to play more interesting rugby.' Coach Hector Mendez was more to the point before the team left for their South African tour in September 1994: 'With the responsibility of having to qualify for the World Cup we have played a conservative game, but now we will endeavour to play more attacking rugby in preparation for the tournament.'

An unsettling fact was that shortly before a thirty-one-man squad was picked to start training in early August for the South African tour, a move by several provincial unions, headed by Buenos Aires and branded as political,

Argentina's front row – Ernesto Noriega, Federico Mendez and Mattias Corral – in the first Test of their tour of South Africa, 1994

Marcello Loffreda, who won his first cap with the Pumas as long ago as 1978, has carried off no less than eleven Argentine championships with his club San Isidro. He is the current Argentine captain

was made to oust coach Mendez and his assistant, Jose Javier Fernandez. It was defeated, but with Union elections at the end of 1994 Mendez could still not feel safe in his job until the World Cup.

About half of the thirty-one players picked for the squad were from outside Buenos Aires and long-distance travelling conspires against squad training. Only one session a week was scheduled before the South African tour with, in the meantime, each player being given a physical training programme to carry out privately. A tour of Australia is marked down for April 1995 and that will have been preceded by the same training difficulties during Argentina's long hot summer. The Australia tour is Argentina's last warm-up before the World Cup as their club season does not start until April.

It is worth noting that only eight of the squad played in the 1991 World Cup – Martin Teran, Diego Cuesta Silva, Guillermo del Castillo, Jose Santamarina, Pedro Sporleder, German Llanes, Federico Mendez and Gonzalo Camardon. Marcello Loffreda, the veteran at thirty-five, was brought back after three years away from international rugby and, as captain, he has provided the experienced leadership which has been missing on the field.

Loffreda has played in the San Isidro club's first division side since 1977 and won eleven championships with them. He made his debut for the Pumas in 1978, but was not in Argentina's World Cup teams of 1987 and 1991. 'I'm not angry about that, because I'm not like that, but I do think we have to learn from our previous errors which were the same in both World Cups. On both occasions too much emphasis was put on the physical aspect and not enough on the rest. There was confusion because it was thought to be more important for the players to concentrate on physical fitness than to develop techniques and tactics and on both occasions many experienced players were left out.'

Players likely to stand out in the World Cup squad are the full-back Santiago Meson, who has recently transferred to Buenos Aires from Tucuman, an excellent kicker who picked up half the points in the four matches against Scotland and the US Eagles in 1994 and who rarely has an off-day; the tall German Llanes, who gains a lot of line-out ball (a previous deficiency for Argentina's not-so-tall team); and the two fast and experienced wingers, Martin Teran and Gustavo Jorge, in the try-scoring department. Another could be Lisandro Arbizu, the Pumas' former captain who missed all last season with injury, and may be back if he regains fitness in time, although he was not included in the original squad.

Argentina's pack won praise for its strength during the 1994 tour of South Africa. The new Springbok coach, Kitch Christie, said: 'They have some fine forwards who make up a very efficient front five. They will trouble several sides.'

Nevertheless, Argentina lost both the Test matches on that tour, although injuries did not assist their cause. Uncertain team selection was also a factor, fly-half Cilley arriving just three hours before the last Test and then scoring a hatful of points to emerge as the star Argentina player on the day. Now they have till May to show that they have settled the formation of their side and can provide an upset in Pool B. They are unlikely to beat England but on form they could certainly give Italy or Western Samoa a game. Against Scotland, on the Scots' tour in 1994, they were far from spectacular, their game plan based on a tedious mauling, forward-orientated style. They certainly have a great deal of international experience but need to develop basic skills and tactics. If they reach the quarter-finals, it may well be considered a successful World Cup for Argentina.

The tall German Llanes played for Argentina in the 1991 World Cup and has been a regular member of the pack since then. His height balances the handicap of Argentina's other not-so-tall forwards

England

FIXTURES

V	**ARGENTINA** May 27, Durban 17.00
V	**ITALY** May 31, Durban 17.00
V	**WESTERN SAMOA** June 4, Durban 20.00

England have a hard job ahead. They should have little difficulty in heading Pool B but could be ambushed by South Africa or Australia, with New Zealand waiting for them if they reach the semi-finals. These games would test the skill and character of any side.

The exchange of views was short and peremptory. England's captain, Will Carling, asked by an English national newspaper journalist shortly before the 1991 World Cup how far he thought his side would go in the tournament, turned the question around. 'How far do *you* think we'll get?' he asked.

Ben Clarke gets the ball away in England's 1994 Five Nations match against France in Paris, won by England 18-14

The interviewer shot back: 'Quarter-finals.' Carling is said to have offered some sarcastic thanks for such little faith. 'You asked my opinion; I've given it to you,' replied the writer.

Four years ago, England defied the critics and went all the way to the World Cup final. True, they missed their date with destiny by failing to capitalise on a golden opportunity to win the famous trophy. But they did at least contest the final. In 1995, even fewer observers of the world game expect them to be involved when the two remaining teams line up for the final at Ellis Park, Johannesburg on Saturday June 24.

Seeing England qualify from Pool B is not the problem. Western Samoa, Argentina and Italy share the pool and none of them looks remotely good enough to threaten a major upset against the 1991 beaten finalists. Argentina were comprehensively defeated in both the recent Tests they played against South Africa, in Port Elizabeth and Johannesburg, in October 1994. They scored tries, won some provincial games on that tour but failed to knock the Springboks out of their stride.

Italy are the minnows of the group, condemned to play their pool games at sea level in Durban, because they lost to Wales in the qualifying competition. The Italians were a crushing disappointment that night in Cardiff and seem unlikely to possess the fire-

Dewi Morris, England's scrum-half, is held back by a South African opponent, in the first South Africa v England Test in Pretoria, 1994

power to disturb England's progress. Nor do Western Samoa, even though they beat Wales in the Pacific last June. The 73-3 flogging the Samoans received at the hands of the Australians will have encouraged England, prior to their meeting in Durban on June 4.

But, if England are expected to breeze through those games, then the next match they will face will be anything but straightforward. The Pool B winners will play the runners up in Pool A – almost sure to be either Australia, the defending champions, or South Africa, the host nation. The prospect for England is an intimidating one.

Kyran Bracken, Bristol's highly promising scrum-half, has been Dewi Morris's deputy in the England team. Behind him is the imposing figure of Brian Moore, England's hooker

Australia seem likely to go into the tournament as clear favourites to retain the trophy. A match with them at the quarter-final stage would be the toughest possible examination of England's credentials. But, if not Australia, South Africa seem certain to bar England's path to future progress. For, unless Canada can provide a major upset, the host nation seems sure to contest with the Wallabies the right to finish first or second in Pool A, based in Cape Town.

The chief problem facing Jack Rowell, the England manager, is that even by June 1995, he will have had all too brief a period in charge of the national squad. The man who steered Bath to the unassailed pinnacle of English club rugby, and kept them there for years, took over when Geoff Cooke suddenly retired at the end of the 1994 Five Nations Championship. Neither Rowell nor anyone else in English rugby had any idea that Cooke would quit before the World Cup. It left a problem for Rowell which has become steadily more apparent as the

Will Carling and Brian Moore bring down a New Zealander in England's impressive defeat of the All Blacks by 15-9 at Twickenham in 1993

relentless countdown to the 1995 tournament has continued.

Rowell recognised, even before he took England to South Africa for a two-Test-match tour in May 1994, that the style the national side was playing was inadequate when faced with the best opposition in the world. What had won the day in the Five Nations Championship was seen to be inferior against the best southern hemisphere sides and their increasingly fast, free-flowing game plan. England had to change, but to implement that change, in both tactics and personnel, in so short a period of time has been Jack Rowell's nightmare.

The recent 1995 Five Nations Championship was supplemented by pre-Christmas friendlies for England against Romania and Canada. That offered Rowell some opportunity for experiment but for the highly astute manager the 1995 World Cup will still come probably twenty-four months too soon. English rugby, under Rowell's urging, had started to show that it recognised the need for change before the 1994-95 season. But the process cannot be achieved overnight just as players will need perhaps two years or more to adopt effectively the new style of play.

Rowell watched carefully as England won and then lost their two Tests against South Africa on their 1994 tour. He has difficult decisions to make in the front row, the back row and at outside half and at centre. Full-back, too, will be another position needing considerable discussion before England launch their campaign against Argentina, in Durban, on May 27. There would appear to be any number of candidates vying for that job – Hull of Bristol, Hunter of Northampton, Pears of Harlequins, Mapletoft of Gloucester and Callard of Bath. But Hunter and Pears have suffered so many major injuries that either would surely be a risk. And Hull's style of play is intrinsically risky. Mapletoft is a newcomer and Callard has yet to cement his claims to the role.

One key decision Rowell must make is whether veteran Rob Andrew is the man to launch the England back-line in the World Cup. Bath's Mike Catt, a South African by birth, has the greater speed and verve but lacks Andrew's vast experience and goal-kicking skills. And if Andrew were to be omitted, who would kick the goals?

Another important choice has to be made at centre. Would Rowell prefer to pair the Bath duo of Jeremy Guscott and Phil de Glanville, rather than include the ageing Will Carling, whose attacking qualities have diminished over the past twelve months? But who would captain England if Carling were not first choice at centre?

The back row is an area of intense speculation. Rowell is known to be worried at the lack of speed in a Richards, Rodber, Clarke back-row unit and may require Bath's Steve Ojomoh for the World Cup in the No. 7 shirt. Or will Neil Back, much maligned for his size, convince the selectors by the end of the Five Nations Championship that he is the right man for the open-side berth? None can doubt Back's pace or bravery, but his small size mitigates against him, especially at the tail of the line-out.

The cover for the first-choice second-row men, Martin Johnson and Martin Bayfield, needs to be significantly strengthened while, in the front row, there are a number of options in all three specialist positions. Will Bath's

South African centre, Brendan Venter, is tackled by Tim Rodber, England's impressive flanker, in the first Test in Pretoria in 1994

Graham Dawe get his long awaited opportunity to unseat Brian Moore from the No. 1 hooker's role? And will the strong young Bath tight-head prop, John Mallett, who played so outstandingly for England on the South African tour in 1994, become the focal point of a new look England front row?

These and several other problems will concentrate wonderfully Jack Rowell's mind before England select their World Cup squad and then head off to South Africa in May. But whoever goes, they cannot escape the fact that reaching the final this time would appear to be a superhuman feat.

They played commendably well against Romania at Twickenham, in November last year, the first international match of 1994-95, but the opposition was exceptionally weak. Now they must accept that, should they overcome either Australia or South Africa in the quarter-final, it is likely that the team awaiting them in the semi-final would be . . . New Zealand. The draw for the 1995 World Cup could have been a great deal kinder to England.

Jeremy Guscott

The world's finest attacking centre, Guscott missed twelve months of rugby in 1993-1994 due to a serious groin injury. He returned to international action in November 1994, winning his twenty-ninth cap in the 54-3 defeat of Romania, against whom he had made his debut in 1989. A free-running, brilliantly creative centre who is also solid in defence, he played for the British Lions in 1989 and 1993 on their tours of Australia and then New Zealand.

Rob Andrew

has now passed sixty caps as England's fly-half. He made his international debut in 1985, against Romania at Twickenham, while still at Cambridge and has now become England's playmaker par excellence. He has also become the side's No. 1 goal-kicker: he kicked all 18 points in England's win against France in March 1994, 27 points for England against South Africa three months later and then 30 points against Canada in December, equalling the world record for points in a match.

Will Carling

was brought into the England side in 1988 at the age of twenty-one and was made captain within the year. He recently made his fiftieth appearance for England by leading them against Romania and has been captain of England longer than any other player. An outstanding, complete centre in his early days, he has in recent seasons lost much of the attacking speed and invention which made him so exciting a player in his youth and early international days. But he seems likely to lead England into the '95 World Cup and remains one of the finest defensive centres anywhere to be seen in world rugby.

Italy

FIXTURES

V	**WESTERN SAMOA** May 27, East London 13.00
V	**ENGLAND** May 31, Durban 17.00
V	**ARGENTINA** June 4, East London 13.00

Welsh fears about qualifying for England's pool in South Africa found only puzzled expressions from the Italians when Wales beat them in Cardiff in the final qualifying match. Italy's 19-29 defeat that night meant that they must join the pool with England, Argentina and Western Samoa. Wales joined New Zealand, Ireland and Japan. But feelings within the Italian camp are that progress is perfectly possible from their group with or without England.

The former Australian international, Julian Gardner, now qualified for the 'Azzuri', although he missed the match in Wales with a knee injury, says: 'It is not a disaster at all that we are in this group. Let's be honest, if you want to progress to the quarter-finals you are going to have to beat some pretty decent sides anyway. Being grouped with England does not frighten us. Every game will be difficult but I don't think any of them are impossible. None of the sides in this group is up to the standard of the leading southern hemisphere nations and, although England are obviously a good side, they do run hot and cold. They are certainly not unbeatable. Argentina are unpredictable and Western Samoa, too, are hard to predict. They blew away Wales in Suva and then were flogged by Australia in Sydney. What do you make

Ivan Franscescato is tackled by the Romanian forward, Lucien Colceriu, in a World Cup seeding match in Catania, won by Italy 24-6. Franscescato, who plays centre for his club, Treviso, is an outstanding scrum-half for Italy. And at Cardiff he played on the wing, scoring Italy's flamboyant try

Diego Dominguez, outside half and champion kicker, must learn to vary his game if the best use is to be made of Italy's dangerous wingers

of that? On paper, England would have to be the favourites but of the others anything is possible. Probably the side that will go through with England will be the one that has been best prepared in the lead-up and has a settled team.'

But, if Italy are to progress, Gardner insists they must eliminate the costly mistakes and indiscipline which hall-marked their performance in Cardiff. 'If we just believe in ourselves at this World Cup that will go a long way to produce that extra twenty per cent of confidence and effort and skill we need. Above all, we have to iron out the fundamental errors; you don't win Test matches by conceding so many penalties. I am optimistic. I think we can do big things and we are certainly capable of producing an upset or two if we gel at the right time.'

There were reasons for the disappointing performance of the Italians in Cardiff. Their well respected captain and back-row forward, Giovanelli, was missing, victim of a serious car crash which puts a major question mark over his availability for the World Cup. The loose-head prop, Massimo Cuttitta, made captain for the night, had just returned from a long seven-week lay-off because of a torn calf muscle and lacked match fitness; the first choice tight-head prop, Properzi, was out with a broken collarbone and the strong second-row man, Giacheri, was another absentee. 'We were all disappointed with the showing of our scrum in Wales,' said Gardner, 'because in Australia on tour a few months earlier, we'd had an especially strong scrummage.'

But, even in Cardiff, there were glimpses of the thrilling attacking style which Italy possesses. Full-back Vaccari is one of the finest players in his position in Europe and there are several other dangerous runners, including Francescato, scrum-half in the 1991 World Cup but a wing when he scored for Italy in Cardiff. The Italians have runners of skill and pace behind the scrum; it is essential they use them.They ought to have sufficient bulk and power up front to deliver that ball, too, so the onus will fall on fly-half Dominguez to get his back line moving. He did not achieve this often enough against Wales although his forwards were not sufficiently assertive always to make that possible.

Dominguez is a champion kicker as he demonstrated by landing eight penalty-goals in Italy's 24-6 defeat of Romania last October. But the twenty-eight-year-old, born in Cordoba, Argentina, kicked too much against Wales and needs to vary his game better if Italy are to utilise their runners out wide. They have the speed and talent to ask serious questions of defences on the flanks, especially from third, fourth or fifth phase possession. It is up to Dominguez to expand their game for, who knows, they might just set Italy alight.

There is no doubt that the Italians have learned better concentration and discipline from their French coach, Georges Costes. Their training sessions are very long and very hard and, as a result, their concentration and fitness have greatly improved. Costes has succeeded in injecting some French flair into the side as well and the results have been really impressive as they were against Australia.

As for Gardner, the former Wallaby just hopes a cruel run of injuries in 1994 will have finally abated in time for him to challenge for a place in the Italian side. 'I would just love to go to a World Cup and I think I could offer the Italians something. I'm thirty now and at my best. I will be working hard on my fitness right up to the tournament and then it's a matter of hoping I get selected. At least if I am fit and playing well, I will have done all that is possible.'

Massimo Cuttitta, Italy's formidable loose-head prop, captained them against Wales in the seeding tournament

Western Samoa

David Lawrenson

FIXTURES

V ITALY
May 27, East London 13.00

V ARGENTINA
May 30, East London 12.30

V ENGLAND
June 4, Durban 20.00

It could be said that the rugby World Cup really came of age as a tournament with the exploits of Western Samoa in the 1991 competition. Just as the African nations captured the imagination in the soccer World Cup, so the Samoans caused the biggest upset in the brief history of the rugby tournament by beating Wales and going through to the quarter-finals.

Having missed out on the 1987 event, few observers knew much about this tiny Pacific island nation and even less about their rugby. All that changed on one unforgettable afternoon at Cardiff Arms Park. Not only did the Samoans prove to be skilful and athletic but they brought something new to the game – devastating tackling. To the Samoans making a big hit is almost as good as scoring a try. Their flanker, Apollo Perelini, earned himself the nickname of the 'Terminator' for a series of big hits which had a shattering effect on the Welsh. Although they eventually went out to Scotland, they had captured the imagination of the public. When they returned home after the tournament, cheering crowds lined the ten-mile route from the airport to the capital.

Apart from the athleticism of their players the biggest asset for the Samoans was their management. Just before the 1991 World Cup they brought in Bryan Williams, the former All Black wing, as a technical adviser. Being based in New Zealand, Williams, who has a Samoan background, not only keeps an eye on the many Samoans playing there but makes sure that the team keeps

Darren Kellett, Western Samoa's young fly-half, is a kicker of world class. Against Wales, during Wales's 1994 summer tour, he even matched Neil Jenkins in the kicking stakes

Brian Lima opens up a Samoan attack during their marvellous win against Wales during the latter's 1994 tour of the Pacific Islands

abreast of current rugby thinking. With the skills of their coach Peter Schuster and manager Tate Simi, this gives the Western Samoan team an edge over their Pacific island rivals.

The win over Wales in the World Cup did not come as a surprise to Bryan Williams: 'We had lots of players who had experience of the New Zealand system and frankly there's no system better. It was just a matter of getting organised. Peter Schuster has a lot of experience and really studies the game. He's a good coach who's well versed in modern techniques.' Their success in the World Cup had its drawbacks as two of their outstanding players, Frank Bunce and Steve Bachop, then switched their allegiance to New Zealand and became All Blacks.

However, Williams is convinced that his team will be even stronger in South Africa: 'We're certainly more experienced than in 1991 and there's lots of young players coming through with plenty of potential. They've been coached in the right kind of techniques and have been learning from an early age. We will be playing a fast-moving, hard-tackling game but we're possibly a bit more structured now than we were. We're kicking for territory and getting good field positions and we concentrate a lot more on ball retention.'

Although Perelini has moved to Rugby League there are still plenty in the Samoan team who are more than capable of inflicting damage as the Welsh found out in the summer of 1994. They were thoroughly outplayed, going down 9-34 in searing heat in Apia. In the young fly-half, Darren Kellett, they have a kicker who is world-class while Pat Lam is a vastly experienced No. 8 and wing Brian Lima has shown himself to be a deadly finisher given half a chance.

However, the Samoans were badly shaken by the mauling they received at the hands of the Australians in July 1994. Although few nations could have lived with the Wallabies on that day, a 3-73 drubbing will have done little good for Western Samoa's confidence.

Their front five remains a weakness, but if they can secure enough ball few will relish facing them in the World Cup. Though England are almost certain to win the pool competition, it is anyone's guess whether Western Samoa will secure a place in the quarter-finals as they did in 1991.

Bryan Williams, Western Samoa's charismatic manager, a former All Black and himself of Samoan origin, is confident that his team will be back to form in South Africa

Pool C

IRELAND	**They have the nucleus of a good side now and hope to progress beyond the group matches**
JAPAN	**Their running game with quick, rapier-like counter-attacks will win them many supporters**
NEW ZEALAND	**1994 ended with some thrilling rugby in the provincial championship. Does the final beckon again?**
WALES	**Injuries to key players disrupted preparation, but they are determined to make the quarter-finals**

New Zealand have to be the favourites to top Pool C and go forward to meet Scotland in the quarter-finals unless, of course, the Ivory Coast, Pool D's dark horses, manage to cause a surprise or two in Scotland's pool. After the All Blacks' massive win at Murrayfield in 1993, an encounter with Scotland should not prove too difficult and so a place in the semi-final, probably against England or South Africa, awaits them. Apart from the huge Test win over Scotland, New Zealand played a disappointing series of Tests against various opponents in 1993-94 until, right at the end of their 1994 season, they put up a tremendous performance against Australia in the second half of the Bledisloe Cup in Sydney. And that was followed by some thrilling rugby in the provincial championship right at the end of the season. The All Blacks' fortunes look really good again.

The second place in Pool C must lie between Ireland and Wales and most critics now appear to back Ireland. They have built up the nucleus of a skilful side, with notable new talents in the shape of flanker David Corkery and the burly hooker Keith Wood, both of whom seem destined to make outstanding contributions to Irish international rugby for many years to come. And they have been unexpectedly strengthened too by the return of Brendan Mullin, a footballer of consummate talent and ability who retired two or more years ago but has now been persuaded to rejoin the colours.

Neil Boobyer, Wales's centre tries to kill a spirited Tongan attack in Teufaiva, June 1994

(opposite) **Richard Loe was a tower of strength for New Zealand in 1991, but he must be doubtful for South Africa**

The crucial match in this pool is obviously the game between Ireland and Wales, the winner of which is almost certain to go through to the quarter-finals. Neither of the two teams can afford to lose: to leave the tournament so early, absolutely empty-handed, would mean a day of mourning for all rugby supporters in the losing country.

Where does that leave Japan, the Asian champions, and the fourth team in Pool C? Probably empty handed too but you never know. At least they are determined to make a bid to stage the 1999 World Cup and they have the infrastructure to make a highly successful job of it.

Ireland

FIXTURES

V	**NEW ZEALAND** May 27, Johannesburg 20.00
V	**JAPAN** May 31, Bloemfontein 13.00
V	**WALES** June 4, Johannesburg 17.00

It is probably an indictment of the disparity in standards of rugby as a world game that Ireland's World Cup will very likely stand or fall completely on the outcome of just one match, the game against Wales in Johannesburg.

Given the composition of Pool C – Ireland, Wales, New Zealand and Japan, the Asian champions – there seems an inevitability about the outcome. None of the other three countries will surely live with New Zealand, a country whose playing levels, not to say aspirations, are miles apart from those of the other nations with whom they are paired.

Similarly, Japan would appear to have won their World Cup battle simply by being there at the finals. To expect them to do anything other than suffer a flogging at the hands of the All Blacks, and then defeats by the Irish and Welsh, would be to stretch fantasy to ridiculous proportions.

But, if Ireland are to prosper, they must win one particular match – the clash with Wales. This, surely, will decide which country accompanies New Zealand into the quarter-finals. Ireland have long been regarded by Wales as a side they wanted to meet in the World Cup. Their *raison d'être* for qualifying in Pool C was their belief that they could topple Ireland. But an Irish side which has shown signs of revival in the last nine months could spring the most unpleasant surprise of all on Wales when they meet in Johannesburg on Sunday June 4.

Ireland have discovered the basis of a talented side, if they can mould together the component parts in time for World Cup action. Newcomers,

Michael Bradley, Ireland's scrum-half and captain in 1993 and 1994 has done much to raise morale after some difficult years

Nick Popplewell, Ireland's formidable loose-head prop, challenges Rupert Moon, Wales's scrum-half, in the Five Nations Championship match in Dublin in 1994

such as their flank forward David Corkery, the twenty-one-year-old from Cork Constitution, and the burly hooker Keith Wood, seem destined to make outstanding contributions to Irish international rugby in the coming years. Both confirmed their rich promise on the Irish tour to Australia in 1994 and, although Ireland lost both Tests to the world champions, good judges, such as the Australian captain Michael Lynagh, praised the contribution of Corkery in particular, who made his life so hard throughout the Tests. His pace to the breakdown, his support play and his fearless work in both attack and defence were some of the reasons why Ireland proved to be so competitive in the Tests.

Ireland used their possession badly in the first Test but in the second, after an Australian massacre looked imminent, Ireland recovered well and Francis scored a try to narrow the gap that had been opened up. In addition to Corkery and Wood – and Bob Dwyer was full of praise for the Garryowen hooker, saying he would soon qualify for a World XV – Gabriel Fulcher and Jordan Bell also made a mark. For Ireland, that tour was an emphatic awakening, showing how very different the game is in the southern hemisphere. Coach Murphy said: 'We have got to go back and make sure we learn the lessons we have just been taught. The game is played differently down here and we must adjust our preparations for the World Cup where the grounds will be even harder and faster.'

As new payers emerge for Ireland, so they hope an old star will spark once again at this World Cup. Centre Brendan Mullin is a footballer of consummate talent and ability, fit to grace any side in the world with his silky skills. Outside Mullin, the flying wing, Simon Geoghegan, should be an even more potent threat after a season in English club rugby with Bath. At full-back, the solid and reliable Conor O'Shea seems just the man for the job.

Up front, Ireland should be able to field a front row capable of living with any set of opponents. Wood as hooker should have British Lion Nick Popplewell as his loose-head prop and Peter Clohessy as tight-head. Behind them, Neil Francis, an enigma wrapped up as a mystery, is still, on his day, one of the world's most effective line-out forwards. There is sufficient talent elsewhere in the pool of forwards available to Ireland – Johns, Robinson, Galwey, McBride, and others – for the selectors to be confident of a ball-winning pack.

Ireland celebrate their great victory over England in the Five Nations Championship at Twickenham, February 1994

Alas, the problem area and indeed the key to the performance of the whole side, may rest on the half-back combination. There is a widely held view in Ireland that the scrum-half, Michael Bradley, and the outside half, Eric Elwood, are simply not quick enough to launch a back line which includes the pace and talent of Mullin and Geoghegan. The selectors will have studied this aspect of their side with care in the 1994 and 1995 Five Nations Championships. Elwood is a fine goal-kicker and Bradley has played his part in raising morale in Irish international rugby after some lean, difficult years. But Bradley's pass is only modest for an international scrum-half and he is by no means the fastest passer of a ball from the base of the scrum. Alain Rolland is much quicker but the selectors stood by Bradley throughout 1993-94 and it may take major pressure through poor results to force a change here.

Three players – David Humphries, Alan McGowan and Niall Malone – have been battling to raise their games sufficiently to put pressure on Elwood for the No. 10 shirt in the national side. Unless the selectors are satisfied that Elwood can release a backline of considerable potential, then they will have to consider one of these other candidates for the job in the World Cup.

Irish international sides usually play with great passion and fervour. In 1987, they reached the quarter-finals before going out to Australia but in 1991 they came within two minutes of providing the upset of the tournament when they led Australia 16-15 minutes from the end. The Wallabies scored once more to escape and went on to win the Cup. But it provided a stark reminder that no one at any time should ever treat an Irish side lightly. Which brings us back to the belief in Wales that to have qualified in the same pool as Ireland should mean a quarter-final place for Wales in the 1995 finals. It may not be quite as simple or as straightforward as that.

Ireland will have received enormous motivation by the knowledge of that frequently expressed view in Wales last autumn. They are never as effective as when their pride is at stake and they appear to have at last sufficient players to raise standards in the their international side. Unlike England or France, Ireland have never been able to field twelve or thirteen world-class players in their international team. Playing resources simply cannot provide that number. But plenty of Irish sides have prospered and indeed won titles by possessing five or six outstanding players and seeing the remainder raise their own game to such an extent that they succeed as a side.

That could yet happen at the 1995 World Cup.

Certainly, if Ireland can reproduce the zip and sparkle that got the better of England in a memorable Five Nations Championship match at Twickenham in February 1994 they should come through. Ireland's try just before half time in that game was special. Ireland won the ball and pushed it forward before releasing their backs. A couple of driving runs in the centre created space for Geoghegan far out on the wing. His speed took him easily past Tony Underwood and through Callard's tackle to the line. It proved to be the winning try and the crowd rose to him.

Only too often Ireland seem to suffer from a lack of ambition or a lack of faith in their abilities. Against Wales at Lansdowne Road in 1994, Ireland failed completely to dominate a game they should have won. Typical of their frustration was the sight of Geoghegan, so desperate for action that at one point he thrust himself into a ruck and started pulling out any red shirts he could find. As one critic said, Geoghegan showed up Ireland's approach: forced to act the bouncer when he should have been their star turn. All Irish supporters will hope that their team play like shooting stars in South Africa, and play consistently for a change.

Conor O'Shea

made his full international debut against Romania in the autumn of 1993 and held the position for the entire 1994 Five Nations Championship. He plays for the Lansdowne club and is one of their chief attacking threats, joining the line from full-back. He had an outstanding tour of Australia with Ireland – his first at senior level – in June 1994, impressing the Wallabies with his cool command and safe defence. He has won only eight full caps yet is already a firm fixture in the Ireland team. O'Shea was unable to make a big impact in the first Test in Australia but showed in other games what a powerful runner he has become.

Simon Geoghegan

is arguably the finest wing in the British Isles and a potent threat to any opponent given his speed and mazy running abilities. He made his international debut in 1991 against France and has been a permanent fixture in the Ireland side ever since. He left his club London Irish to join the English champions Bath at the start of the 1994-95 season and has shown distinct signs of raising his standards even higher, doubtless a comment on the standards pertaining at Bath. He has now passed twenty senior caps for Ireland.

Brendan Mullin

returned to international rugby against the USA in November 1994 after a self-enforced retirement period dating back to the Five Nations tournament of 1992 when he suddenly announced he was quitting the international game. Mullin made his senior debut for Ireland back in 1984 against Alan Jones's Australians and then represented Oxford University in 1986-87. The holder of forty-six caps, he has been an outstanding attacking centre-threequarter of high skill. His return in the autumn of 1994 was ruined by an injury which forced him to miss the entire second half of the USA match. But he is a key man in Ireland's World Cup plans.

Japan

Alvin Sallay

FIXTURES

V	WALES	May 27, Bloemfontein 13.00
V	IRELAND	May 31, Bloemfontein 13.00
V	NEW ZEALAND	June 4, Bloemfontein 15.00

Qualifying for the World Cup was simply the first battle won. The real war begins now. During the 1995 World Cup the Japanese Rugby Union will be making a very strong bid to host the 1999 event. 'If we had not qualified for these finals, it would have been silly for us to have bid for the 1999 tournament. But now we are here, we will be staking a claim at the next IRB meeting,' said Shiggy Konno, Japanese rugby's strong man, who is leading his country's campaign.

Japan became the last nation to qualify for South Africa, when they defeated their arch-rivals and historic foe South Korea 26-11 at the Cheras Stadium in Kuala Lumpur, after a match in which they were always in control. So after more than seventy qualifying games all over the world, the final piece in the World Cup jigsaw was slotted in. Japan will play against New Zealand, Ireland and Wales in Pool C in Bloemfontein.

Happy to have kept alive their proud record of having taken part in the finals of every World Cup, the Japanese are now eagerly looking forward to mounting a publicity campaign in South Africa in support of their bid for the 1999 tournament. 'We have all the infrastructure in place already to host a major event like this', Shiggy says. 'When there were doubts about South Africa being able to host the 1995 event, we offered to host the tournament then. Preliminary studies had been made and a contingency plan was in place. It will be simple now to go ahead and make a bid,' he added.

Bruce Ferguson, Japan's big lock forward from Fiji, is the third of their "foreigners"

A country which boasts the most modern facilities - stadiums, telecommunications, hotels - will have no problem in playing host to one of the world's major sporting events.

To add credibility to their claim, the Japanese can proudly say that they are truly the flag-bearers of rugby in Asia. In 1987, for the first World Cup, they were invited to represent Asia and they lost all their matches. In 1991 they beat only Zimbabwe in the tournament, but in South Africa they will hope to go one better and perhaps claim the scalp of either Ireland or Wales. It will not be easy for them. Even the presence of three overseas-born players, the Tongan back-rowers Sinali Latu and Sione Latu (no relation) and the Fijian lock forward Bruce Ferguson, will hardly turn the Japanese into a potent force. They do not have the big forwards capable of winning them quality possession. And the game plan which they have adopted of late will see them struggle against bigger and taller opponents.

The former England lock Paul Ackford, in Kuala Lumpur in his new

Tsutomo Matsuda, Japan's full-back, with the speed to turn a defensive position quickly into attack

capacity as rugby writer for the *Sunday Telegraph*, put it succinctly: 'It surprises me to see Japan playing a European game. They should concentrate on their strengths and rely more on quick hands and passing rather than trying to play with the forwards. They might be big compared to the rest of Asia but in the World Cup they will come up against bigger forwards,' warned Ackford.

Japanese rugby is at the crossroads. They don't know whether to play with their forwards, or to play their traditional running game. If they could only evolve a style combining the best of both games, they could spring a surprise in the World Cup. They will rely heavily on their three "foreigners" to try to do this.

'Everyone draws attention to our three "foreigners" but they have lived in Japan for a long time,' points out Shiggy. Sinali came to Japan in 1985. He is a tweny-nine-year-old flanker, who works for Sanyo, represented Japan in the first two World Cups and has also played against the All Blacks, Scotland, Fiji, USA and has toured Argentina and Wales. He has won twenty-seven caps and is one of the most experienced players in the side. The No. 8 Sione has been in Japan for four years, while the Fijian-born Bruce Ferguson is the newest of the trio, having arrived only in 1993.

'If we wanted, we could field at least ten top expatriates in the national side, and still stay within the IRB requirements,' claims Shiggy, 'but then it would no longer be a Japanese side. We won't do that. We will place a self-restriction and play only three expatriates in the World Cup.'

Of the home-grown players, the most experienced, who featured prominently in the Asian Championship final, is the dashing winger Yoshihito Yoshida. With the looks of a movie star (in the early days of his career, he was mobbed by his female fans after every match), the twenty-five-year-old Yoshida scored both his side's tries against the Koreans.

Watch out too for the long-haired full-back from the Toshiba corporation, Tsutomo Matsuda. Rock-solid in defence, Matsuda has the speed to contribute greatly to the Japanese ability to turn a defensive position into attack. This will be their main weapon - the lightning quick, rapier-like counter attack. Against Wales, on the disastrous 1993 tour, played out largely in mud and rain and wind, there was little chance of rapier-like attacks of any sort and in the Test they succumbed to their hosts by the record score of 5-55.

However, if this ploy works for them in South Africa, they might be able to take their next objective - to do well there. Then, who knows, the war could be won and they could find themselves hosting the 1999 World Cup.

Sione Latu, Japan's Tongan-born No.8, played well in the Asian Championship

New Zealand

Keith Quinn

FIXTURES

V	**IRELAND**
	May 27, Johannesburg 20.00
V	**WALES**
	May 31, Johannesburg 20.00
V	**JAPAN**
	June 4, Bloemfontein 15.00

If you had asked a New Zealander in August 1994 what he thought of the All Blacks' chances of winning the 1995 World Cup, you would have been met by a pretty long face. New Zealanders were despondent about their cup-winning hopes. In six Tests that year, the All Blacks had won only two, drawn one and lost three. Now, however, they are all smiles again with a real hope of winning the World Cup with a team graced with speed and outstanding skill.

The reason for the turnabout was the thrilling quality of their play in the second half of the 1994 Bledisloe Cup against Australia and in the national provincial championship. Week after week all over the country the top six or so teams played a quality of football that was truly astonishing. All-action explosive backplay was mixed with committed and driving forward work to make a blend of high-speed rugby not seen in New Zealand before. The skill factor of all the players was as high as anyone could remember. Only the jungle of line-out play seemed not to have improved.

The standard was so good (with the exception of the dismal brawling championship final) it begged a couple of obvious questions. How come the All Black players who trudged their way through six grim Test matches in 1994 were later transformed into such twinkle-toed provincial players? And have the All Blacks' selectors, Messrs Mains, Kirton and Copper, noted those same players' change of mood? If they can transfer the new provincial style into the All Blacks' Test teams, then, mark my words, New Zealand will win the World Cup.

More than anything, the thrilling national championship promoted the cause of several new young players who should be pushed forward now to permanent All Black status. As they used to say in New Zealand, 'paste these names in your hat' – Glen Osborne, Waisake Sotutu, Tabai Matson, Jeff Wilson, Lee Stensness and Andrew Mehrtens. All were youngsters who seized their moments brilliantly. All must now go close to selection for World Cup matches.

Osborne in particular is a sizzling counter-attacking North Harbour full-back who has been recognised at Sevens play before but who must surely play for his country in the next year or two. Wilson, who was the All Blacks' teenage star on the tour of England and Scotland in 1993 but who faltered after injury at the start of the 1994 season and played only one Test, was back to his scorching best late in the season. Wilson's try for Otago against Auckland was a kick and chase and dive of enormous skill and thrill.

Stensness was another young All Black who played superbly late in the season as a midfield back. Matson and Sotutu are both Fijian-born threequarters who are strong and powerful runners, while Mehrtens (South African born incidentally) is a gifted young five-eighths player who, though still prone to the occasional wrong option, is a must for the future.

Laurie Mains, back as the All Blacks' coach after a dogged struggle for the position with former coach John Hart, has been saying little about the composition of his first national training squad for summer preparation for the World Cup. Pressure is mounting for him to make changes in his thinking to include the kind of inventiveness which so marked the late-season championship games.

Unwittingly perhaps, Mains himself discovered the new style which so captivated late season rugby watchers in New Zealand. In the Bledisloe Cup Test against Australia in Sydney in August, his team was behind 6-17 at half-time. Mains faced a personal crisis. To lose the game by a big score would surely have seen him lose his national coaching place. Mains walked grimly towards the All Blacks' half-time huddle in Sydney and presumably gave the team the word to attack flat out in desperation in the second half. The All Blacks responded with easily their best and most bursting play of the season. The Aussies were caught short on Test-match fitness but still hung on to win a thriller 20-16. The same style of total attacking game plan was then reproduced by the provinces for their remaining championship fixtures.

Mains claims he held back on several tactics during the 1994 Tests so

Walter Little goes round Australia's David Knox in the Bledisloe Cup match in Sydney, August 1994

***(opposite)* Lee Stensness scores for the All Blacks in the Test against Western Samoa, won 35-13 by New Zealand, in Auckland, July 1993.**

as to keep some things away from the prying video eyes of World Cup opponents. Not everyone believed him but now Mains has the chance to facelift his Test side. There are cries for him to move aside such veterans as Richard Loe, Mike Brewer, Frank Bunce and even the captain, Sean Fitzpatrick, to make way for a new page in All Blacks history.

Mains has proved during his time with the All Blacks to be a conservative coach so it is unlikely or unreasonable to expect him to drop all the above but the question remains – even at this late stage – has Mains the courage to make his Test players play with the freedom and youthful fervour the provincial coaches did? Can he help them to play again as they did against Scotland at Murrayfield in November 1993?

Admittedly, the Scottish team was appallingly weak on that occassion. But even so, New Zealand played with the speed and relaxed ease of a training session. It was a near-perfect display. New Zealand went ahead in the third minute and were still on all-out attack when the final whistle was blown. The score was 51-15, New Zealand's highest for a full international in Europe, and Scotland conceded 50 points for the first time in their 122-year Test history. And the All Blacks' Jeff Wilson became the youngest player to score a hat-trick of tries on his international debut.

The reasonable judges who had sad faces in August are now saying with some degree of confidence that if Mains does make some alterations and brings in the best of this year's youngsters then a scorching All Blacks team could blow away all their opponents in South Africa, certainly those in Pool C – Ireland, Wales and Japan – with sheer speed, fitness and skill and the trophy would be theirs. All New Zealand supporters hope the All Blacks will show the world that their rugby is alive and running once again.

Blair Larsen, the All Blacks' lock, is challenged by West Hartlepool's John Dixon, playing for the Northern Division against the All Blacks during their 1993 tour of England and Scotland.

Jeff Wilson

was the All Blacks' golden boy on their 1993 tour of England and Scotland, and scored a hat-trick of tries on his Test debut against Scotland at Murrayfield in the All Blacks' crushing 51-15 victory. He represents Otago and is still only twenty-one. He has also represented New Zealand at cricket against Australia and played for Southland at both cricket and rugby when still at school. He can play wing or full-back.

Sean Fitzpatrick

has captained the All Blacks, in succession to Gary Whetton, since 1992. He first played for New Zealand in 1986 and has now passed sixty caps for the All Blacks. Tough, hard and durable, he has been at the core of Auckland's many internal triumphs in New Zealand rugby for most of the last ten years and has played well over one hundred matches for the country's most successful provincial side.

Wales

FIXTURES

V	**JAPAN** May 27, Bloemfontein 1300
V	**NEW ZEALAND** May 31, Johannesburg 2000
V	**IRELAND** June 4, Johannesburg 1700

On the night when Wales's long, wearying journey on the road to the 1995 World Cup finals came to an end at last, two sets of differing emotions were to be perceived at Cardiff's National Stadium. As the Welsh celebrated their 29-19 victory over Italy to decide which group the respective sides would join in South Africa, watching representatives from Ireland's squad were almost equally happy at the outcome.

It was always Wales's intention to reach Pool C in South Africa, as Europe's top qualifier. There, they knew, they would share the company of New Zealand, Ireland and the Asian qualifier, Japan. It seemed crystal clear to the Welsh that a place in this group offered them the realistic possibility of finishing runners-up to New Zealand, thereby securing a quarter-final place.

Thus, after Wales had won in Romania and then beaten Italy in Cardiff, there was a huge, collective sigh of relief throughout the Welsh camp. The only trouble was that the Irish, on the evidence they had seen before them that night, were wearing smiles just as wide when they left Cardiff. For the Irish were far from impressed with Wales's victory over the Italians. Indeed, it was only the kicking of fly-half Neil Jenkins, who booted 24 of their 29 points, which ensured a Welsh win. And the Irish quietly smiled at the prospect of meeting, and beating, Wales in Pool C, based in Bloemfontein and Johannesburg.

Beyond dispute, Wales still have considerable problems to overcome before they begin their campaign in South Africa. Serious early season injuries to their captain Ieuan Evans and first choice full-back Mike Rayer, both of whom suffered broken legs, and the defection of the inspirational Scott Quinnell to the Rugby League

Tony Clement bursts down the wing in Wales's seeding match against Romania in Bucharest, 1994

Rupert Moon passes out under pressure during Wales's great victory over France at Cardiff in the Five Nations Championship, 1994

champion club, Wigan, left Wales wondering who would fill those critical roles, especially if Evans and/or Rayer should be unable to regain fitness and form in time for the World Cup. Swansea's Tony Clement, used on the wing as a replacement for Evans against Italy, would step up at full-back as Rayer's deputy. But Wales have plenty of other difficulties to overcome before they can anticipate beating anyone in the finals, including Ireland.

The Welsh line-out was obliterated by the Romanians in Bucharest in 1994 and that area has to be strong and operating productively at World Cup level. The dispute over who plays at scrum-half is also likely to rumble on right up to kick-off time in the tournament. Rupert Moon is a bold, brave, committed player who fills well enough the role of extra back-row forward in the way he takes on opponents. But he does not possess the class of Swansea's British Lion, Robert Jones, and it remains a mystery to rugby men throughout Britain how and why Wales came to omit a performer of Jones's proven quality. The Welsh are not exactly bursting with world-class players at this moment in their history. Jones, who is certainly in that category, is a player who would launch their line and enable them to play the game wider out, which should be the ambition of every side in South Africa.

Wales have an adequate, if far from intimidating, pack of forwards. Cardiff's giant 6ft 10in second-rower, Derwyn Jones, seems to be a man to contribute mightily to their line-out and the New Zealand-born back-row man, Hemi Taylor, another Cardiff forward, also looks like becoming a vital member of the side.

Fly-half Neil Jenkins will also be critically important for his prolific goal-kicking. But, if Wales believe they can rely solely on his boot to produce wins in the World Cup, they may be sadly misguided. Wales have to expand their game plan and Jenkins must show he can do more than simply kick goals all through a match. If he can distribute and set up attacks as well, especially in broken play, players further out such as Nigel Davies, Mike Hall and the flying

wing, Nigel Walker, could demonstrate the exciting potential that they undoubtedly possess. Clement, too, comes readily into this equation.

But bad luck has already dogged the Welsh so much during 1994 that the coach Alan Davies and manager Robert Norster will need to show inspirational qualities to get their men in the right mood. Wales will surely beat Japan, the Asian champions, and surely lose to New Zealand, which will make the match against Ireland, in Johannesburg on Sunday June 4, the one which will probably decide the last qualifying place for the quarter-finals. Neither country would have it easy in the last eight for the French are likely to be awaiting the winners of the Celtic clash. But for both sides, reaching the quarter-finals of the tournament is the minimum requirement. Should they get there, even a defeat by the French would be accommodated. But defeat at the pool stage, and subsequent early return home, would be classed as an ignominious failure.

At the first World Cup in 1987, Wales finished an outstanding third after beating Australia in the play-off match. Alas, their fortunes had slumped dramatically by the time the second World Cup was staged in 1991. Their failure to beat Western Samoa in Cardiff meant that they went out at the group stage, having to watch the Samoans contest a quarter-final with Scotland in Edinburgh. Western Samoa beat them again, by 34-9, in Apia at the end of Wales's long and exhausting tour of Canada, Fiji, Tonga and Western Samoa in June 1994. Coming after the runaway victories gained over Spain and Portugal as Wales went through the formality of qualifying for the World Cup finals, the end of their summer had been a hard one. And then in the autumn they had to face matches against Romania and Italy to make sure of the place in Pool C they wanted. In the Five Nations Championship the

Gareth Llewellyn, the Neath captain, leaps high in the line-out to win the ball for Wales. Llewellen may be Wales's captain in the World Cup if Ieuan Evans fails to recover full fitness in time

previous spring they had unexpectedly finished top of the table, albeit only on points difference, after losing to England at Twickenham. But they had had an outstanding win over France in Cardiff and it seemed then as if their nightmare of failure was coming to an end. However, they did not play well against Romania at the start of the seeding competition, suffering perhaps from the exceptional heat, and some would say they were lucky to win. But there was little noteworthy action and the game's only try was another Ieuan Evans gem, with which he broke the record for the number of international tries scored by a Wales player.

Against South Africa at Cardiff in November 1994, after the Springboks had demolished Scotland the previous Saturday, Wales fought well and were far from humiliated when the game ended at 16-9 to South Africa. Indeed, as the game entered its final quarter, Wales took the lead with a Neil Jenkins penalty. If their injured players can recover their fitness and form before the World Cup begins, Wales are capable of qualifying from their pool and making a real impact on the tournament.

However, if Wales were again to fall at the pool stage without even sniffing quarter-final action, the gloom which has lingered for so long over the Welsh valleys would instantly return. The players understand fully the implications for the country of success or failure at this tournament.

Ieuan Evans

The charismatic captain of the Welsh international side, Ieuan Evans has been dogged by injuries in recent years. His latest setback has been a broken leg which denied him the leadership of his country against South Africa in Cardiff last November. Evans is a brilliant attacking wing whose try helped Wales beat Romania in the crucial World Cup qualifying tournament in Bucharest in September. He plays for the Llanelli club, and is one of the few true world-class players currently available to Wales. He played for the 1993 British Lions in New Zealand, and made his international debut in 1987 against France. If he plays in South Africa this May and June he will appear in his third World Cup competition.

Hemi Taylor

Originally from New Zealand, Hemi Taylor has played in Welsh club rugby for several years, principally with the unfashionable Newbridge club. However, when he became eligible for the Wales national side through residency qualification, he switched to Cardiff and has greatly impressed during the last twelve months. Able to play anywhere in the back row but most effectively at blind side flank, he made his debut for Wales in the World Cup qualifying match against Portugal last summer. A strong, committed, driving type of forward whose support for the ball carrier and workrate make him extremely valuable for any side. He had a fine game against South Africa in Cardiff at the end of the Springboks' tour in 1994 and should win many more caps.

Derwyn Jones

The biggest forward in Welsh rugby at 6ft 10in and 18st 7lb, Derwyn Jones has made considerable progress under the shrewd guidance of the ex-Australian forward coach, Alec Evans, at Cardiff. He has played for Neath, Llanelli and the English club Northampton in 1992, the latter while he was studying at Loughborough Colleges. But he settled at Cardiff and then played for Wales 'A'. An increasingly effective line-out performer, he made his full debut for Wales against South Africa at Cardiff in November 1994.

FFR

Pool D

FRANCE	**Excellent discipline is France's new trademark and they are some people's tip as champions**
IVORY COAST	**Ivory Coast's great triumph has been simply to qualify: it's a wonderful boost for African rugby**
TONGA	**Tongan rugby has improved enormously in recent years and no team can take them lightly**
SCOTLAND	**If, as they should, Scotland beat Ivory Coast and Tonga, they will be assured of a quarter-final place**

It is difficult to see anyone pushing France off the top of Pool D. They used to be feared for their unpredictability; now they are respected as a hard, disciplined, well organised team while retaining the kind of flair which can suddenly turn a game upside down. Though a number of outstanding performers of the recent past have now retired, the French can still draw on some fine players – Sella, Cécillon, Cabannes, Benetton, Lacroix and the mercurial Roumat among others. The captain is the dependable Saint-André and the full-back, Jean-Luc Sadourny, Blanco's successor, has few peers in the world as a sound tackler in defence and a speedy runner in counter-attack.

Scotland, once again captained by Gavin Hastings and about to prepare for his third World Cup, have played Tonga not so long ago on their Pacific Islands tour, and of course have experience of France, whom they meet each year in the Five Nations Championship. Scotland are going through a period of rebuilding, especially after their massive defeat by the All Blacks at Murrayfield in 1993, where they lost also to France in the Five Nations and to South Africa in 1994.

France win a scrum against Australia during their 1990 tour down under. A growing number believe that France could win the 1995 World Cup

***(opposite)* Gavin Hastings cleverly keeps the ball available to release colleagues during the Scotland v France Five Nations match at Murrayfield, 1994**

Tonga were invited to take part in the 1987 World Cup but lost out to Fiji in 1991 and are now back again at Fiji's expense. Since those earlier days, Tongan rugby has greatly improved. Their coaching is good and many of the players who have gone overseas to play, mainly in Australia and New Zealand, have brought back the considerable lessons they have learned to help the local players.

The fourth side in Pool D, the Ivory Coast, are the real dark horses. No one expected them to survive the African qualifying tournament at the expense of Namibia, Zimbabwe or even Morocco. But Duncan Paterson, the Scotland team manager, who attended the finals in Casablanca, reported back with enthusiasm on the sheer size and athleticism of the Ivory Coast players. Just to have arrived in South Africa is a tremendous success story for African rugby.

France

Henri Bru

FIXTURES

V	**TONGA** May 26, Pretoria 18.00
V	**IVORY COAST** May 30, Rustenburg 18.00
V	**SCOTLAND** June 3, Pretoria 17.00

Will the French go on blossoming in June? For three years now it has been by far their favourite month. Test series won in Argentina, South Africa and New Zealand in three successive years have done much more for their reputation than ordinary performances in the Five Nations Championship during those winters.

France's captain, Philippe Saint-André, is tackled by Tim Horan and Jason Little when France beat Australia 16-13 in Bordeaux, 1993

One of the main objectives of Pierre Berbizier when he was appointed France's coach in early 1992, after their disastrous showing in the second World Cup, was to make his team worthy opponents for sides in the southern hemisphere. In that he succeeded, the world champions Australia going down in Bordeaux in October 1993. And it is not the only area in which the former scrum half has made his mark. Everybody acknowledges the huge improvement made by France in team discipline, a sector which used to be their Achilles heel.

Discipline on and off the field has never been France's trademark. They used to give away at least 12 points to any opponents for blatant infringements when they were under pressure. And opponents and referees were too well aware of that weakness to let it go. Now it seems to be a thing of the past, though an outburst of the old bad habits is always possible. But, considering what did happen in top games against the Springboks, Wallabies and All Blacks, there is some reason to be optimistic. Even under the most extreme pressure, France did not give away silly penalties and points along the way in those games and that makes life more difficult for their opponents. You do have to score your points from your own moves against the French now.

France used to be feared for their unpredictability. Now, they are respected as a hard, disciplined, organised team while still retaining the inspired French touch, the kind of moves which can turn a game round as they did in New Zealand in 1994 in the second Test by scoring a try three minutes from the end after a move spanning the whole pitch.

It is fair to say that they no longer have top-class players such as Blanco, Lagisquet, Berbizier or Rives. But the general feeling is that as a team, they are stronger than in the past, less subject to ups and downs. They now make defence the best platform for attack, and concentrate more on the basics: possession, kicking, playing for position. But the fire is still sleeping under the ashes, and it can always flare up in a second.

Step by step, they have created, with the World Cup in mind, a well organised team, able to cope with any kind of opposition. They have built what is needed to reach the top: a solid platform in the forwards, a good goal-kicker, and once again discipline.

The rest of the rugby world seems to have been slow to notice the new France. Most of the stories about the French still refer to their unpredictability, their flair, and all those other clichés. Berbizier will not try to destroy that illusion: it is quite an advantage to be seen like that, but the surprise factor will not last especially when coaches start looking closely at videos.

Of course, seen from abroad, there are still some signs of *la différence*. Philippe Saint-André, for example, is France's fifth captain since 1992, his predecessors being Sella, Cécillon, Tordo and Roumat. But that just means that, in the French culture, the position of captain is not as important as it is in a British team. Turnover of players can be sometimes more important than it is in British teams. But France, with their 200,000 rugby players, can probably afford that luxury more than a country with more limited resources.

A lot of names in the French squad will ring a bell for every viewer. First among them is the incredible Philippe Sella, still going really strong

Olivier Roumat wins a line-out against Wales in the 1994 Five Nations Championship match in Cardiff

at thirty-three and with more than one hundred caps behind him. He has been the rock on which France's backplay has been anchored for years, a fearsome defender, and a danger for any side. Alongside him comes Philippe Saint-André, not especially quick, and not a fashion model on the pitch, but a competitor, always at the top when he needs to be. And a guy like Thierry Lacroix is very underrated: look at his percentage of successful goal-kicks in big Tests and you will be surprised.

Jean-Luc Sadourny, the full-back, has a very difficult task in following Serge Blanco in the No. 15 jersey. He is not the same kind of player as the great Blanco, but so far as fielding the

France's Laurent Cabannes evades a tackle by Canada's No. 8 Glenn Ennis during the France v Canada Test in Ottawa, in June 1994, lost by France 16-18

garryowen, counter-attacking or tackling soundly in defence are concerned he has few peers in the world.

Up front, both the huge Moroccan-born Philippe Benetton, a hard-nose tackler who is always well positioned, and Laurent Cabannes, an all-round performer, are outstanding. Line-out ability, tackling capacity, smartness in the open, physical strength: what one of them does not manage, the other achieves. They have played a major part in the successes of France abroad in the past three years. Cabannes, especially, is one of a rare kind, a back in the forwards, or a forward in the backline when needed. Not a big guy by physical standards, but he survives the big challenges.

And then comes the mercurial Olivier Roumat. On his day, he can be one of the best jumpers in the world: safe hands, leg strength and cleverness. Alongside him the huge Olivier Merle can do the donkey work with his great weight and all the strength accumulated by seven years as a shot putter. He has gained a lot of experience in only two years, and the jokes which were made about him when he began his rugby career are quickly vanishing as his performances continue to improve.

More important, this French team has proved it can reach its peak after three to four weeks together. Their historic victory in two Tests against New Zealand in June 1994 sent a warning

The French front row against Australia at Bordeaux, 1993: (right to left) Armary (of Lourdes), Gonzalez (Bayonne), and Seigne (Merignac)

signal to all the other World Cup contestants: France is alive and well! Rarely, if ever, has any team worked so hard on tour. They won the first Test 22-8 in Christchurch and squeezed the second by 23-20 in Eden Park, Auckland. In an unrelenting physical struggle, France never gave up. They trained for five hours every day and all were supremely fit. They probably soaked up more punishment, tackled harder and longer, and stuck to their game plan more than any other French side has ever done. At the same time, the final match-winning try, scored by their full-back Jean-Luc Sadourny two minutes from the end, after a move which had started in France's 22, was unforgettable. It was a try almost good enough to be set beside Blanco's in the World Cup of 1987.

Moreover, the World Cup schedule has been quite lenient to them. Warm-up games against Tonga and the Ivory Coast before meeting Scotland should lead to either Ireland or Wales in the quarter-finals. If everything goes according to plan, France will not have to meet one of the top teams before the semi-finals, nearly four weeks into the competition, and should not have had to dig too deep into their reserves. And from then on, given their unpredictability, they will not be easy meat for anybody.

Philippe Sella

of Agen and France became the first player in history to win one hundred caps for his country when he played for France in the first Test against New Zealand in Christchurch in June 1994. A powerful centre, Sella will be thirty-three when France play Tonga in their first World Cup match in Pretoria. As fit as ever, he made his international debut far back in 1982 against Romania and has been virtually ever present in the French side since then. His strong running in attack has made him a difficult opponent to stop and his ability to remain on his feet in the tackle has been a key element in France's ability to maintain continuity in their play in recent seasons. Sella's contribution to his club side Agen has been long recognised as outstanding.

Philippe Saint-André

was thrust into the captain's role in the French national side for the final match of the 1994 Five Nations Championship season, after shock defeats for the French by Wales and England. This charismatic character immediately inspired those around him to such an extent that France ended the season by breaking a long run of failure at Murrayfield by beating Scotland. A mazy, unpredictable wing who is hard to pin down, Saint-André typically started the movement which led to France's winning try in the second Test against New Zealand last June, from inside his own 22. A member of the Montferrand club, Saint-André made his international debut in 1990 against Romania at Auch.

Jean-Luc Sadourny

had the unenviable task of taking over from the immortal Serge Blanco, France's former captain, in the full-back shirt of the national side. The Colomiers player made his international debut in 1991 as a replacement against Wales and has remained virtually ever present in the French team. He has developed into one of the most elegant, classical full-backs in world rugby. His running in attack, in support of colleagues, has been a feature of French back play and he remains cool and commanding in defence, particularly under the high ball. He is destined to become one of the world's greatest players.

Ivory Coast

FIXTURES

V	**SCOTLAND** May 26, Rustenburg 1600
V	**FRANCE** May 30, Rustenburg 1800
V	**TONGA** June 3, Rustenburg 1300

Everyone thought they were only there to make up the numbers. And even those who had travelled to watch the African nations qualifying tournament in Casablanca did not bother to give the Ivory Coast a second glance. Until, that is, they had qualified to play in South Africa.

Then, shock and astonishment was everywhere to be seen. Two nations, Namibia and Zimbabwe, were the favourites to fight it out for the one qualifying place available. In the end, perhaps they concentrated too hard on each other for, behind their backs as it were, the Ivory Coast slipped in to steal the spoils and will be lining up alongside France, Scotland and Tonga in Pool D, playing all their games in Rustenburg.

When they began the qualifying tournament by losing 9-17 (three tries to nil) against Morocco, even the Ivory Coast's few followers wrote off their chances. But this was to be a strange and turbulent qualifying competition in which everyone beat everyone else. Morocco beat the Ivory Coast only to lose to Zimbabwe who had lost to Namibia, who then themselves lost to the Ivory Coast but the crucial game was the last one between Morocco and Namibia. It finished in a 16-16 draw but, if Morocco had landed one of the late penalties they missed, they, and not the Ivory Coast, would have gone to South Africa.

Athanase Dali is Ivory Coast's playmaker and fly-half and shared the goal-kicking with the full back Soulama in Casablanca. He also captained the side in that tournament

Watching the extraordinary scene was Scotland's team manager, Duncan Paterson, who had flown out to Casablanca for some early viewing of whichever country emerged to take its place in the same group as the Scots. Paterson found the whole experience unforgettable and was mighty glad he had taken the trouble to go to Casablanca. What he saw convinced him that Scotland can, in no way, take lightly the challenge of the Ivory Coast in South Africa this summer but also that an African nation is set to make almost as significant a mark in Rugby Union as countries such as Nigeria and Cameroon have made in soccer's recent World Cups.

Paterson said: 'The Ivory Coast will not be straightforward opponents for us or for anyone else in South Africa. They are a very big, physical side and will cause problems to all the teams they meet. They may have been a little naive in their tactics in the qualifying tournament because after they won the ball they tended to kick it away too much. But I expect them to have ironed out many faults like that by the time they play in the finals. These guys will be very proud men in South Africa. We can expect them to play above their usual standard. They will be doing anything but making up the numbers and no side that plays them can afford to take that sort of attitude on the field. A lot of the Ivory Coast players are playing in France anyway and are being exposed to high standards.

'I was not watching specific individuals. For me the thing that stood out was the sheer size and athleticism of the Ivory Coast players. They will be very physical in the World Cup, making big tackles like the Western Samoans and other Pacific Islanders. A side playing them must be ready for that. They only really let themselves down with one or two silly kicks which wasted possession. But they will learn from their mistakes and one thing they certainly do have is ball-winning potential. Technically, they appear to have a tight scrum and there are plenty of big men able to win line-out ball. They also have a quick back row which makes strong tackles. If they were all playing their rugby regularly at a higher standard, they would make terrifically fast progress. I am just glad I went to see them play. At least we will be ready for them now.'

Fly-half Athanase Dali captained the Ivory Coast in the qualifying tournament and shared the goal-kicking duties with the full-back Soulama. The prop-forward Djehi is the tough man up front, providing strong scrummaging skills. The side was coached by Dominique Devanier and Claude Ezoua and they instilled a strong team spirit which served the side well in difficult moments during the qualifying tournament.

Toussaint Djehi, the Ivory Coast's formidable prop, who plays his club rugby in France, is in the centre of the picture

Few expect the Ivory Coast to win a single match in South Africa. Their achievement has been to get there. But the other nations in their group might do well to heed Paterson's warning. A light-hearted approach is not advisable against the tournament's rank outsiders. With so many of the side playing in France it has not been easy to arrange training sessions since their Casablanca triumph. However, a training-camp was organised in Strasbourg in November 1994, including a match against the Strasbourg club and that important get-together proved well worthwhile.

The Ivory Coast's scrum-half during their energetic training-camp in a dank and misty Strasbourg in November 1994 was Frédéric Dupont, who plays his club rugby for Nimes

Scotland

Bill McMurtrie

FIXTURES

v **IVORY COAST**
May 26, Rustenburg 16.00

v **TONGA**
May 30, Pretoria 20.00

v **FRANCE**
June 3, Pretoria 17.00

Scotland were fourth in the 1991 World Cup. Since then, though, results have not been to their liking. Even the aura of being seemingly invincible at home has gone, and Scotland's stock plummeted with the 15-51 defeat by New Zealand at Murrayfield in November 1993.

Too many wise old Scottish heads have retired since 1991. Sean Lineen, David Sole, John Jeffrey, Finlay Calder, and Derek White left the international scene more or less together, and, worst of all, a severe knee injury to Gary Armstrong meant that Scotland have to go into the World Cup campaign without arguably the best scrum-half in the world.

Yet, nothing ventured, nothing gained. The Scots were the first to declare their hand in stating categorically who would lead them in the World Cup. With the tournament still eight months away, Scotland's selectors named Gavin Hastings as captain not just for the Five Nations Championship but also for the world tournament in South Africa in May and June.

Hastings was naturally delighted with the nomination and confirmed his relish for the challenge that lay ahead. Even if he were not to play in every match before the World Cup his appointment gave Scottish rugby a focus. At the time of his appointment – the third successive year Hastings had been nominated for the duration – he had fifty caps to his name. So had his brother, Scott. They were only two short of the Scottish record held by two Hawick players, Jim Renwick and Colin Deans, and Gavin at least was set up for the rare distinction of playing in

Scott Hastings tries to get a pass away to his brother Gavin in Scotland's Five Nations match against France at Murrayfield, 1994. Yanne Delaigue is the France No.12, winning his first cap

Tony Stanger of Hawick, who has won more than twenty caps on the right wing for Scotland, looks to get a pass away to his centre

three World Cup tournaments. Scott was expected to share that honour even though, because of injury, his participation in the 1987 World Cup was confined to only a few minutes against Romania in Dunedin.

That year the Scots drew 20-20 with France and then beat Zimbabwe and Romania before losing to New Zealand in the quarter-final round. Four years later Scotland successively defeated Japan, Zimbabwe, Ireland, and (in the quarter-final) Western Samoa before going out to England – all five matches played at Murrayfield – before they fell once again to the All Blacks, this time in the third-place play-off in Cardiff.

Scotland might have expected to meet Zimbabwe for the third successive tournament, but the Ivory Coast put paid to that notion. The former French colony won the African qualifying tournament with victories against not just Zimbabwe but also Namibia. When Scotland open their campaign against the Ivory Coast in Rustenburg on May 26 it will be the first time the two countries have met. Indeed, the West Africans have never aspired to play against any of the rugby world's old establishment.

With foresight, however, Scottish cards have been marked about the Ivorians. Duncan Paterson, Scotland's team manager, was in Morocco for the qualifying tournament, and he came home with respect for the Ivory Coast players' physique and strength. The Scots will not under-estimate their first 1995 World Cup opponents, even though they will naturally expect that their own expertise and experience will be more than enough to see them comfortably over the first hurdle.

Craig Chalmers, the Melrose stand-off, a pillar of strength for Scotland since 1989, lost his place to Gregor Townsend during the 1994 Five Nations Championship. Will he be Scotland's first choice at outside half for the World Cup?

Scotland lost narrowly to England in the semi-final of the 1991 World Cup and disappointed all their supporters. Here Mike Teague, the England flanker, gets the ball away from the scrum

Scottish rugby has more experience of their other Pool D opponents, Tonga and France, especially the latter. The Scots and French have been allies for centuries – Mary Queen of Scots, after all, ruled one while being, briefly, consort of the other's king – and the countries have been rugby rivals for close on ninety years.

For a long time neither could win on the other's ground – until France broke their Murrayfield bogey in March 1994 – and even when they met on neutral territory in the 1987 World Cup the result was a draw. What a memorable match it was that day at Lancaster Park, Christchurch. It had a sparkling start with Finlay Calder's break for Derek White's try. It had Serge Blanco's cheeky try off a tapped penalty while Matt Duncan was lying on the ground having attention to injury (play was meant to stop for such reasons in those days). It had, too, that late try by Duncan to tie the scores, but Gavin Hastings missed the touchline conversion for victory. France won the group by scoring three tries to two in that match, which meant that Scotland had to meet New Zealand in the quarter-finals. Scotland lost 3-30.

Scotland's tour of Argentina in the summer of 1994 was less than successful. For all sorts of reasons they had to make the journey with a largely inexperienced squad, little better than an 'A' team in fact. They managed to beat only one moderate provincial side and lost both Tests, though narrowly, by 15-16 and 17-19. These were Argentina's first victories over Scotland for twenty-three years. By then Scotland had played no fewer than eight international matches without a win. In the 1994 Five Nations Championships they lost to Wales, England and France and could only draw with Ireland.

Scotland take on the Ivory Coast and Tonga before they meet France, and fortunately they have recent experience of the Pacific Islanders. This comes from their 1993 tour through Fiji, Tonga and Western Samoa, when the results, even by a squad well short of international honours, generated confidence that was rudely shattered by the All Blacks at Murrayfield six months later. Scotland did not award caps for the final game against Western Samoa. The two victories in Tonga, however, including 23-5 in the Test, were worthy results, and both matches provided appreciation of the fast, physical game the Scots can expect in Pretoria on May 30.

Gregor Townsend took most of the blame from coach Douglas Morgan for Scotland's performances in the two Tests in Argentina, and few doubted that trusted lieutenants in the shape of Craig Chalmers, Tony Stanger (though he has said he wants to play in the centre in future), Rob Wainwright and Doddie Weir would be back well in time for the World Cup. Morgan believes that one positive lesson learned from that tour is that a country like Scotland should undertake a full tour only every other year and that in between the SRU should concentrate on a development tour. Certainly the Argentine visit, though unsatisfactory at Test level, proved that certain players, when confronted with challenges greater than Scotland's domestic rugby can normally provide, do respond positively.

New discoveries were the scrum-half Derrick Patterson, now playing his club rugby in England with West Hartlepool, and Duncan Hodge, of Watsonians and Edinburgh University, the youngest member of the party, was the controlling influence in Scotland's win over Cordoba. And it was Hodge whose drop-goal won the match for Scotland 'A' against South Africa during the Springboks' autumn tour of Wales and Scotland.

It is clear that Scotland have much to do before setting out to win their pool games in South Africa. They were a bitter disappointment to their fans in the full international against the Springboks at Murrayfield last autumn. Their defence frequently collapsed against the speed and power of the South African backs and their tackling generally was woeful.

In South Africa, if Scotland win their pool, they will face a quarter-final against Wales or Ireland; if they finish second, they will once again play a World Cup tie against New Zealand.

Bryan Redpath

has been the long-term scrum-half understudy to Gary Armstrong, who suffered another severe knee injury early in the 1994-95 season, giving Redpath a chance to press for the World Cup position. He is the youngest of three brothers, all of them having represented the same Melrose team. Bryan represented Scotland at Under-18 and Under-21 levels and has been a key player in Melrose's Scottish championship successes in the last two years. He made his international debut as a temporary replacement during the 1993 international against New Zealand at Murrayfield and toured Argentina with Scotland in 1994.

George Weir

has played a key role in the way Melrose has dominated the Scottish game in recent seasons. George ('Doddie' to everyone) Weir can play second row or No. 8 although his height (6ft 6in) and mobility are rather more impressive than his bulk (15st 6lb) and work at close quarters. He has now passed twenty full caps for Scotland, but has also represented Scottish schools, Under-19, Under-21 and Scotland 'A'. He comes from a strong rugby family, both his brother and his father having played for Gala.

Andy Reed

is a Cornishman who qualifies for Scotland through his mother, who was born in Edinburgh. Reed, originally from St Austell, came to prominence with England's champion club Bath and has had a meteoric rise into senior rugby. He made his international debut for Scotland in 1993 against Ireland and was immediately chosen for the British Lions tour of New Zealand that year, playing in the first Test. He captained Scotland on their tour of Argentina in the summer of 1994 and has become an important member of the senior Scottish pack.

Tonga

David Lawrenson

FIXTURES

V	**FRANCE** May 26, Pretoria 18.00
V	**SCOTLAND** May 30, Pretoria 20.00
V	**IVORY COAST** June 3, Rustenburg 13.00

Tonga were the only side invited to the inaugural World Cup in 1987 who missed out in 1991. But they're back for the South African tournament at the expense of their South Seas rivals, Fiji, whom they beat on aggregate over two matches.

Tonga are probably the least known of the Pacific island rugby nations. They produce big, strong, athletic rugby players but the country is desperately poor so most of the better players move to New Zealand and Australia.

Moreover, because of the national team's lack of success over the years, it has become increasingly difficult to entice these players back to play for the national side. Success in the World Cup, however, could transform the island's fortunes just as it did for Western Samoa in 1991.

To assess the potential of Tongan players you need to look no further than the Wallaby flanker, Willie Ofahengaue. A member of the World Cup winning Australian side, Tongan-born 'Willie O' is one of the most dynamic back-row forwards in world rugby. Significantly he was back in Tonga during the summer of 1994, helping to coach the national team prior to their game against Wales. Although they went down 9-18 to the tourists, there was enough evidence to show that they cannot be taken lightly.

The match against Wales was decided on penalties with Neil Jenkins winning the kicking duel with Sateki Tu'ipulotu, but the young Tongan full-back showed that he was an accomplished kicker who could cause the opposition problems. The Tongans won a lot of ball at the front of the line-out thanks to their impressive lock Falamani Mafi, who plays his club rugby in Canberra and who dominated the front of the line against Wales.

Evidence of the improvement in Tongan rugby came in the annual triangular tournament when, although they lost narrowly to Samoa, they beat Fiji by 12-10 to secure a place in the 1995 Super-10 series. This provided both an enormous financial boost for the struggling Tongan Union and the

Manu Vunipola passes out from the scrum during Tonga's match against Wales, June 1994.

Falamani Mafi, who plays his club rugby in Australia, is halted by a Welsh defender during Tonga's match against Wales, June 1994

opportunity for an excellent build-up to the World Cup. Fiji took an early lead in that game but the Tongan forwards fought well to draw level with a try by their captain and hooker, Fe'ao Vunipola, converted by Sateki Tu'ipulotu. Fe'ao Vunipola is one of three brothers in the side. He believes that Tongan rugby is getting better: 'The coaching has improved but the most important thing is that the players who have gone overseas to play have brought their experience back to assist the local players. I played for Wellington for three years, and the standard was so high. In Tonga, you sometimes see players walking to a line-out and I have to push them to run.

'Our game is similar to Samoan rugby – we like to play it physical. We just run straight, get the ball back and hit again. We've also tried to improve our scrum and line-out, which is the basis of the game. Anything is possible in the World Cup if you put your heart into it. Samoa beat Wales in the last one by running at them so we need to put in some big hits.' Against Scotland, in June 1993, the Tongans lost 5-23 in Nuku'alofa, scoring a single try through Lavaka, and the following month were heavily defeated by Australia, 14-52, so there is a lot of ground to be made up. Even so, there is reason to suppose that standards have improved during the last eighteen months.

Fe'ao's brother Manu is the only survivor from the squad which went to the 1987 World Cup. 'It was great because I'd only seen most of the teams and the players on television. I particularly remember playing against the Welsh who had Jonathan Davies and Bob Norster in their side.'

For the game against Wales in 1994, Tonga were missing a number of overseas players who had declined to return. Coach Sione Taumoepeau says this is a problem: if they did make themselves available for South Africa then his team could cause an upset. 'It's good for them to play overseas because the intensity of our club games and the provincial scene here is nil. But it does cause us problems as far as big-match preparation is concerned and these players are the core of the side. We play a fast, rucking type of game whereas Europeans try to maul – especially under the new laws. So we'll try not to tie the ball up too much because most of the European teams are strong in the upper body. I think we are in a good group for the World Cup. We've got the Ivory Coast and Scotland, who were strong when they were down in the South Seas in 1993. France, of course, on their day could be world champions but on another. . . you never know.'

Fe'ao Vunipola, Tonga's hooker and captain, makes a break for Tonga during their match against Wales, June 1994. Wales won 18-9

WORLD CUP GROUNDS

POOL A	**NEWLANDS, Cape Town**	**Capacity 50,000*** used for Western Province Currie Cup matches	Pool matches *(May 25, May 30)* plus one quarter-final *(June 11)* and one semi-final *(June 18)*
POOL A	**BOET ERASMUS STADIUM, Port Elizabeth**	**Capacity 34,000** used for Eastern Province Currie Cup matches	Pool matches *(May 26, May 31, June 3)*
POOL A	**DANIE CRAVEN STADIUM, Stellenbosch**	**Capacity 17,000** Stellenbosch University Ground	Pool match *(June 3)*
POOL B	**KING'S PARK, Durban**	**Capacity 51,000*** used for Natal Currie Cup matches	Pool matches *(May 27, May 31, June 4)* plus one quarter-final *(June 10)* and one semi-final *(June 17)*
POOL B	**BASIL KENYON STADIUM, East London**	**Capacity 15,500**	Pool matches *(May 27, May 30, June 4)*
POOL C	**ELLIS PARK, Johannesburg**	**Capacity 62,000** used for Transvaal Currie Cup matches	Pool matches *(May 27, May 31, June 4)* plus one quarter-final *(June 10)* and the final *(June 24)*
POOL C	**SPRINGBOK PARK, Bloemfontein**	**Capacity 36,500*** used for Orange Free State Currie Cup matches	Pool matches *(May 27, May 31, June 4)*
POOL D	**LOFTUS VERSFELD, Pretoria**	**Capacity 50,000** used for Northern Transvaal Currie Cup matches	Pool matches *(May 26, May 30, June 3)* plus one quarter-final *(June 11)* and play-off for 3rd/4th place *(June 22)*
POOL D	**OLYMPIC PARK, Rustenburg**	**Capacity 30,000**	Pool matches *(May 26, May 30, June 3)*

* Anticipated capacity when extensions and rebuilding completed